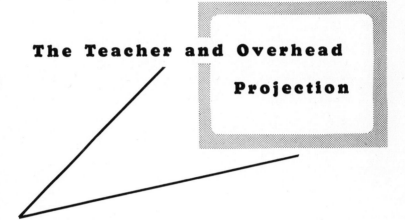

The Teacher and Overhead Projection

The Teacher and Overhead Projection

Projection

A Treasury of Ideas, Uses and Techniques

MORTON J. SCHULTZ
Technical Communications Consultant
Author of *Photographic Reproduction
Methods, Techniques and Applications
for Engineering and the Graphic Arts*

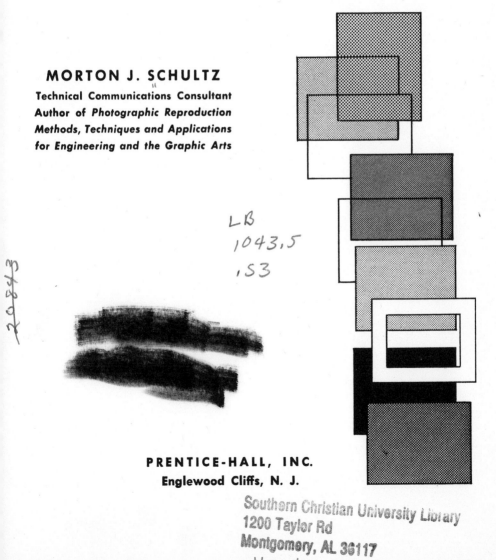

PRENTICE-HALL, INC.
Englewood Cliffs, N. J.

Preface

Using overhead projection to teach is not a new concept. It dates back to World War II when the armed services employed overhead projectors for teaching recruits. These earlier projectors, and those that found their way into classrooms after the war, were large, cumbersome devices that presented as many drawbacks as advantages.

Modern projectors, however, offer none of the disadvantages of older models and, at the same time, amplify utility. They are light in weight, easy to use, and permit utilization in fully lighted classrooms. Furthermore, they permit the teacher to face the class at all times.

Why are projectors of such great value to educators? Many reasons will become apparent as you read this book, but it should be noted at the outset that a projector is a visual aids tool. It is not designed to replace the teacher, but instead increases capability since we know that children learn faster and better when they are able to see subject matter as well as hear it.

There is another important aspect of projection that should be noted immediately, although this too will become vividly clear as you read. Overhead projection saves the teacher her most precious of all commodities: time. Lengthy chalkboard dissertations and hours spent reproducing material for a classful of students by another process are eliminated when a teacher has a projection capability at hand.

As you study the examples of projection use presented in this book, two definite facts will become apparent:

1. The use of the overhead projector in teaching is limited only by the imagination of the teacher.

2. Although your interest in teaching might center itself on a particular subject area, the value of the experiences of teachers in other subject areas can be of immense assistance. For example, the way in which a teacher of mathematics makes use of pro-

jection might indeed be applicable to your use, although your teaching field is history. Furthermore, teachers should keep in mind the importance of approaching subjects that are presented via projection from the aspect of cross-disciplines, especially in the elementary grades.

The author is especially grateful to the 3M Company of St. Paul, Minnesota, for its invaluable assistance in the preparation of this book. Much of what is presented between these covers is a result of a nationwide search by the 3M Company in the firm's Assistance Grant to Education program for uses of projection by the in-class teacher. Some 15,000 proposals were submitted to 3M from schools across the nation for judging by a panel composed of educators. The ones presented in this book are not only those which were judged to be of a superior nature, but also those of a less luminary nature which the author felt were necessary for emphasizing particular points concerning projectors and projection.

The author also wishes to acknowledge the assistance given by the many educators to whom he went for help. He can't name all, but wishes to point to two in particular—both teachers. They are his wife, Janice Peck Schultz, and her mother, Mrs. Matilda Peck. Their guidance was invaluable, and although this book would have probably been prepared without it, any measure of success it does achieve must be shared with them.

In conclusion, the author must stress an obvious fact. This book is a reference volume in the true sense of the word. It is a book that should be used. The reader can get maximum advantage from it by referring to its pages when the need arises, just as he or she refers to any teacher's aid.

For Your Convenience in Using This Book

Since the purpose of this book is clearly that of assisting the teacher in doing a more effective job, any material contained in this book may be duplicated by the teacher for classroom use.

In addition, a list of the names and addresses of suppliers of the various materials mentioned throughout the book can be found in the Appendix on page 229.

Contents

The Teacher and Overhead Projection

1.

Transparency Overhead Projection —
the Teacher Oriented System

How often has a teacher been faced with this problem? He has a
piece of material he wishes the class to see. Perhaps it's a map, or a
written document, or a diagram depicting the electrolysis of water, or a
sentence structure, or any one of a number of things. He wants the
students to see it, because it will help to clarify a lesson for them. Yet,
passing the material around would take too much class time, and dupli-
cating it by ditto or any other process to get the number of copies
required would take too much of the teacher's time. Thus, the material
is either placed on a bulletin board which is anything but desirable,
or it's returned to the file.

This is the way it was, but it need not be so any longer. With the
development of the overhead projection technique, you—the teacher—
have available one of the most effective methods for communicating
visually with your class.

Four pieces of equipment provide you with a complete capability
for overhead projection in the classroom. These are the overhead projector (Figure 1.1), an infrared copying machine for reproducing black-
and-white original material in black and white (Figure 1.2), a white-light
copying machine for reproducing both black-and-white and colored
originals in black and white, (Figure 1.3), and a screen. Only two, however, are actually needed for effective visual communication in the
classroom—the projector and one of the copying machines. Since
material can be projected onto a blank wall, not even a screen is needed,
although it is best to use one for maximum image resolution and clarity.

Figure 1.1. This is the typical overhead projector in use in many schoolrooms throughout the country. Incorporating new concepts in optical design which are tailored to meet the wants and needs of the teacher, its major characteristics include compactness and light weight, easy positioning to provide unobstructed viewing, and ease of operation.

Figure 1.2. The desk-top size infrared copying machine features automatic exposure control, automatic on-off control, and transparencies ready for projection in just four seconds after exposure of transparent film to original.

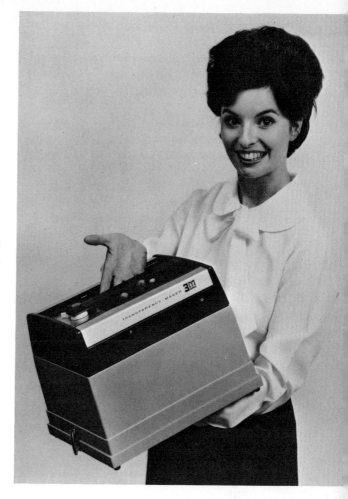

Figure 1.3. The lightweight white light copying machine incorporates many of the features of the infrared machine, plus the additional capability of being able to reproduce colored originals in black and white.

Five Terms You Need to Know

Before discussing the characteristics and usage of each piece of equipment employed for overhead projection, it is necessary to define five terms which are basic to an understanding of projection and, therefore, to an understanding of this book. These terms are *original, reproduction, transparency, positive,* and *negative.*

An *original* is the piece of text or illustrative matter that you wish to project for viewing. It could be a map, graph, test paper, newspaper clipping, magazine page, drawing, or what have you. It is the material in the form in which it was originally printed or prepared by a lithographic or printing process, by an artist or draftsman, by a student, or by you.

Examples of originals include a picture from a magazine showing cactus for a geography course, a letter written by a student for a course in handwriting, a bar graph showing the relationship of average temperatures of various cities in your state for a course in science or mathematics, a list of subjunctive verbs for a foreign language class, and headlines cut from a newspaper to show various types of headline construction for a course in journalism.

A *reproduction* is the term applied to a piece of material which is transferred or copied from its original state to an intermediate state. For overhead projection, an original is copied onto a sheet of transparent film, which is the intermediate stage between the original and projection. (A complete discussion of these films is presented in Chapter 2.) This copying process is performed by means of a copying machine which simply transforms lines, words, drawings, and so forth from the original onto the reproduction medium.

With some older types of overhead projectors, it is not necessary to make a reproduction for projection. The opaque original can be laid directly on the projector and the image will be cast. However, aside from this one advantage, there are no others offered by the so-called opaque overhead projector, as will be pointed out later in this chapter. Thus, this book is designed primarily to acquaint you with the uses and advantages of the transparency overhead projection system.

A *transparency* is the sheet of transparent film on which a reproduction of an original is made. The original material you desire to project is laid in contact with the sheet of film and the two are passed through a copying machine where the transparent film is exposed, thus transferring the image from the original onto the film. It is this transparency which is laid on the overhead projector for viewing by your audience. A transparency can be in either positive or negative form.

A *positive* transparency reproduces the image of the original in terms of gray or black. For example, suppose you have a map composed of black lines that you wish to reproduce. By placing the original in contact with a sheet of *positive* transparency film and running them through a copying machine, the result will be a transparency consisting of black lines—in other words, an exact duplicate of the original.

A *negative* transparency is one that reverses the light representation. For example, an original with a black line illustration becomes, via negative film, a black background with a white line image. It is similar to the ordinary film negative you make every time you take a picture with your camera. On your negative, black tones of the original subject are reproduced as clear areas, while light tones are reproduced as black areas. When the negative is placed in contact with a sheet of sensitized photographic paper and exposed to light to make a picture (*a positive*), the exposing light readily passes through the clear parts of the negative. Hence, the sensitized paper beneath receives more exposure and darkens. The same exposing light does not, however, pass as readily through the dark parts of the negative. Thus, the paper beneath receives less exposure and stays lighter. The same principle can be applied to an understanding of negative transparencies.

Suppose, for example, you have an original document upon which is printed a bar graph in bold, black ink. You want to show this to the class, but for an unusual effect you wish to have the bar graph reproduced as a clear image on a dark background. This is done by placing the original into contact with a sheet of *negative* transparency film and running both through a copying machine. The resultant transparency will show a clear image area (often referred to in photography as a white image area) on the background. The reproduction, in other words, is a reversal of the original and will appear as such when projected.

Overhead Projector Design
Emphasizes Simplicity and
Ease of Use

The transparency overhead projector, the heart of the system, is a comparatively simple device which is available in various models. It is light in weight, easy to operate and focus, and provides projected images of the highest resolution and clarity.

To operate the projector, you simply center the transparency on the machine's glass stage, so the transparency is right-reading—in other words, so you look down and read the words on it in the normal manner—and flip the on-off switch.

The projector operates off an ordinary 110 to 125 volt alternating current wall plug.

Most of today's projectors range in weight from about 15 pounds to about 40 pounds, depending on the model. The so-called classroom and meeting room projector, specifically designed for classroom work, is only about 15 pounds in weight and measures approximately 14 inches by 14 inches by 27 inches (Figure 1.1). The heaviest projector weighs about 40 pounds, but is designed primarily for auditorium use and is, therefore, a more or less permanent installation (Figure 1.4). There is

Figure 1.4. This type of projector, which is the so-called auditorium model, is used more or less for permanent installation in a large room, such as an auditorium. Weighing only about 40 pounds, however, it could be used in any room should the need arise.

Figure 1.5. The portable overhead projector utilizes a carrying case for ease of portability. It can be set up in seconds by opening the case and elevating the optical head.

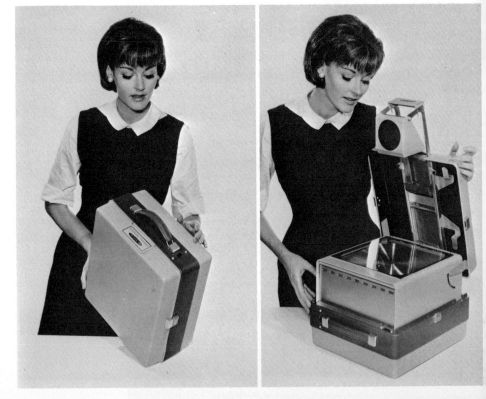

also a portable model available which weighs about 20 pounds. It is equipped with a self-contained carrying case for ease of portability (Figure 1.5).

If we are to consider the overhead projector as the heart of the transparency overhead projection system, we must consider the copying machines as the arteries that feed the heart. These machines are used to produce the positive and negative transparencies from the original material. There are two types available for use in the classroom: the infrared copying machine and the white-light copying machine.

The infrared copying machine is the famous "Thermo-Fax" brand machine which has been used for many years in offices to make duplicate copies from original material. To make transparencies with this machine, you simply place the transparency film in contact with the

Figure 1.6. Original and transparency are fed into the infrared copying machine and, in just four seconds, you have a perfect transparency reproduction for projecting.

original, adjust the exposure dial to provide the desired image density, and place the original and film into the machine's feed (Figure 1.6). The machine exposes and "develops" the transparency. It is a dry developing process in that no liquid chemicals are used.

The main disadvantage of the infrared copying machine is its inability to reproduce colored originals in black and white. It can only produce a black image of an original onto positive transparency material as black or onto negative transparency material as clear (or white). However, transparency materials are available for use in the infrared machine which provide a colored background for the black or clear image (Chapter 2). It is also possible to add color to the reproduction yourself by means of grease pencil, overlays, color adhesive films, and other devices which will be discussed in detail throughout this book.

The advantages of the infrared machine are its ease of operation and speed in reproducing material. The simple, one-step reproduction process takes only four seconds from the time the original and transparent film are fed into the machine to the production of the finished transparency.

Generally, if your requirements call for the quickest and easiest method of making transparencies and you seldom have to reproduce colored originals, then the system you need would probably be the overhead projector and the infrared copying machine.

The white light copying machine offers more reproduction flexibility than the infrared machine, but does not have the latter's operational advantage. With this type of copier, you can reproduce both black and white and colored originals in black and white.

Reproduction with the white-light copier is a multi-step process. Generally, you must expose the film and then develop it to make a transparency (Figure 1.7). It is a dry developing process. The entire procedure from exposure to finished transparency takes some 40 seconds, as compared to the four seconds needed to make transparencies with the infrared machine.

Thus, you should consider use of the white-light copier if you need a full transparency reproduction capability that includes reproduction of colored, as well as black and white originals, into black and white reproductions.

There is still another reproduction capability open to you, and this is reproducing full color originals in full color by means of the so-called

Figure 1.7. The white light copying machine produces a finished transparency of any color in black and white in about 40 seconds. The carrying case, which also doubles as the exposure unit, is lifted from the base which serves as the developing unit (top left). The original and an intermediate sheet are placed beneath a glass plate contained in the base, and the exposure unit is fitted over the plate (top right) to make an exposure of several seconds. The intermediate sheet and a sheet of transparency film are then placed together in the developing unit (lower left). In a few seconds, the image forms (lower right). The teacher can check it visually to see when the correct stage of development has been reached, stopping the process whenever the result is satisfactory.

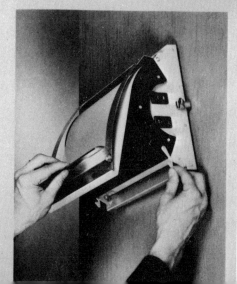

color lift process, which involves use of the infrared copying machine. A discussion of color lift is offered in Chapter 2.

Six Steps to Effective
Visual Communication

Overhead projection has been welcomed by the teacher as a valuable addition to the classroom. It is designed to supplement the teacher, not replace him. The teacher's enthusiasm and approach to teaching are actually enhanced by use of this visual communication tool. For this reason, the overhead projector has been termed a "teacher-oriented machine" by the teachers who have used it.

Immediately, one can recognize several advantages in using overhead projection in the classroom. These are as follows:

1. The teacher faces the class at all times and speaks directly to the students while projecting material on a screen in back or to the side of him (Figure 1.8). Naturally, this is not possible when using a chalkboard since the teacher's back must be to the class while writing. Nor is it possible with older type opaque overhead projectors which have

Figure 1.8. This is one of the things that is meant when we say overhead projection is a "teacher-oriented system." The teacher faces the class at all times while material is projected. This is impossible to do when using the chalkboard.

to be placed at or near the *rear* of the room for proper focusing on a screen in front of the room. With the opaque machine, the teacher talks to the students' backs and not directly to them, as she does when employing the transparency overhead projector.

2. The transparency overhead projector can be used in a completely lighted room. Projected images can be seen clearly by all students, including those in the last row, no matter what the size of the class-room or how brilliantly it is lighted. There is no such advantage with an opaque projector. In using an opaque projector, the room must be completely darkened, since the presence of light affects the visibility of the projected image.

3. Once a transparency is made, it is permanent. It cannot be ac-cidentally erased, as can a lesson on a chalkboard. Nor will a trans-parency fade with usage or time.

4. The projector is light enough in weight to permit easy carrying from classroom to classroom. An opaque projector, on the other hand, is a heavy piece of machinery that often requires placement on a caster-equipped table for rolling from room to room. In the absence of such a table, many teachers would have to call a custodian, whose other duties might prevent immediate response. Thus, a lesson would either be delayed or would have to be presented without the aid of a projector.

5. The teacher is able to maintain complete classroom control and interest in a lesson by simply turning a switch on and off. When you wish to direct student attention to you, you turn the projector off. When you wish to direct attention back to the visual material, you turn the projector on.

This is one of the most important points to keep in mind when using the overhead projector: to maintain absolute control over class atten-tion, *use the on-off switch*. It is one of the best devices at your disposal which, when employed in a judicious manner, will help you to maintain complete control over the lesson and over student reaction to that lesson.

6. The teacher can supplement the transparency with several devices and techniques to further enhance interest in a lesson and maintain attention. Some of these devices and techniques are the pointing method, using a transparency as a chalkboard, the revelation tech-nique, the silhouette technique, the projection of transparent objects, the use of colored transparent tapes and sheets, and the use of over-

lays. These and others will be depicted vividly in the chapters to follow
by calling upon actual case studies of how the transparency overhead
projector has been used by teachers throughout the country. However,
the following principles basic to an understanding of these techniques
are presented for your edification:

• *Pointing.* After you have made a transparency from any teaching
material, a simple way of drawing attention to the item you wish emphasized on the projected image is by using a pointer. A pointer can be
any opaque object placed on that portion of the transparency under
discussion. It is placed directly on the transparency, which is on the projector stage. The pointing object casts a shadow image on the screen
(Figure 1.9). A pencil, pen, or even your finger can serve as the pointer.
The pointing object should be rested on the projector stage to eliminate
movement.

• *Chalkboard technique.* The overhead projector can be used in
place of a chalkboard, thus providing you with more versatility than
that offered by the latter. A grease pencil is used in lieu of chalk and a
clean, unexposed sheet of transparency film is used in place of the chalk-

Figure 1.9. Although you
use overhead projection, the
long - established teaching
practice of pointing is not
impeded. It is actually enhanced.

Figure 1.10. Since transparency materials can be written on and erased, you can make effective use of overhead projection as a chalkboard device.

board. The film is put on the projector stage, and the grease pencil is used to write directly on the transparent material. As you write, the image is cast upon the screen for the students to see (Figure 1.10).

You can imagine the possibilities afforded by this technique. Suppose, for example, you wish to demonstrate the solution to an algebraic problem in a step-by-step manner, with the class participating in the discussion. You can begin by placing a clear transparency on the projector stage and writing the problem on it. As each step in the solution to that problem is discussed, it can be written on the transparency. If a mistake is made or you wish to eliminate a portion of the problem, the grease pencil can be erased by wiping the transparency with a soft rag. The class sees the way in which the problem evolves, but what is equally important is that you have your eyes on the students at all times and can determine by their reaction whether they comprehend the lesson.

Using the principles involved in this technique, you can make a transparency from an original piece of copy containing a test that has been prepared in advance. The transparency is placed on the projector stage for viewing by the students who are taking the test. The advantage here is that you don't have to take class time in writing the test out on the chalkboard; nor do you have to take time to prepare copies of the test by ditto or another reproduction process.

• *Revelation technique.* This technique is one of the most important offered by the transparency overhead projector, because it enables you

Figure 1.11. Revealing information bit by bit is one of the most effective of all teaching methods to aid students in retention of material, to keep them from being distracted by information not yet presented, but revealed, and to enhance their interest. The overhead projector is ideally suited for this practice.

to employ, as does no other means of visual communication, one of the most effective teaching methods known. Revealing projected material to a class bit by bit is a psychologically sound way to attract attention to the subject. An opaque sheet of paper is the simplest revelation mask you can use. Placed over all or part of a transparency, it blocks out the area you do not as yet wish to reveal to the class. As you go from point to point, you can uncover the topic of the moment for revelation to the class (Figure 1.11). If you wish to cover up the material already revealed, while keeping material not yet discussed under cover, you can use several strips of opaque paper or specially shaped masks. At the beginning of the lesson, everything on the transparency is covered. As the first point is discussed, you remove the mask covering the applicable material on the transparency. When you have completed discussion of the point, you replace the mask and then proceed to the next point. In other words, nothing but that material under discussion is revealed at any one time.

● *Silhouette technique.* This technique employs the same principle as that used in revelation. The principle is:

Any opaque object placed on the stage of the transparency overhead projector casts its shadow outline on the screen.

Thus, you can project shadow pictures you wish the class to see in a simple, but dramatic fashion (Figure 1.12). Some of these pictures could be triangles, circles, squares, rectangles, map outlines, lettering outlines, or what have you.

Specifically, biology teachers can show leaf specimens very satisfactorily for comparison or identification by placing these leaves side by side on the projector stage and casting their images on the screen; drawing and geometry teachers are able to do constructions more readily with conventional drawing tools by means of silhouetting with the overhead projector, thus obviating the need for special enlarged tools employed with the chalkboard. For that matter, any teacher who teaches by means of equipment, including manipulative equipment, can make use of the projector as a silhouetting device.

• *Projecting transparent objects.* A number of tools and devices, such as slide rules, straight rules, triangles, and protractors, are available in transparent form. When placed on the stage of the projector, these are clearly projected onto the screen (Figure 1.13). You can see the value of this technique if, for example, you were instructing a class on the use of the slide rule.

Figure 1.12. Objects silhouetted by means of the overhead projector are interesting and attractive to students and aid in their education.

Figure 1.13. Transparent tools placed on the overhead projector are clearly projected onto the screen to become fully visible to students. This permits the teacher to show the uses of these tools in problem solving.

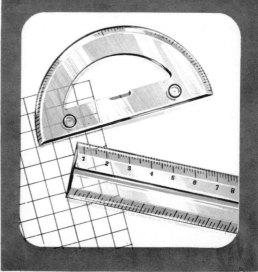

• *Use of colored transparent tapes and sheets.* Transparencies can be supplemented with colored transparent pressure-sensitive tapes. A wide variety of widths and colors, both plain and patterned, are available. Graph work is especially suited to the use of this material (Figure

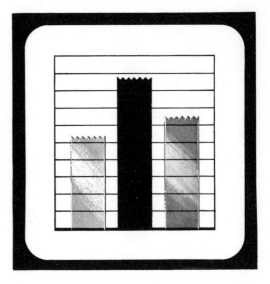

Figure 1.14. Being transparent themselves, colored pressure-sensitive tapes cast their colored images onto the screen when projected.

1.14). Colored plastic sheets can be used to provide a full-color background to a transparency.

• *Overlays.* This is a particularly effective technique for presentation of material in a step-by-step fashion. Information which lends itself to this type of presentation is information that can be broken down into component parts. A transparency is made of each component, and then the component transparencies are taped together or to a frame in proper registration. Registration refers to the placement of the component parts of the broken transparencies, so that when all components are put together they are accurately emplaced in relation to one another. The series of components are then flipped into place on the stage of the projector as the information is developed (Figure 1.15).

For example, suppose you wish to show the geography of the state of New Jersey, depicting its rivers, mountain ranges, and major cities. To show this to a class using the overlay technique, you would first have

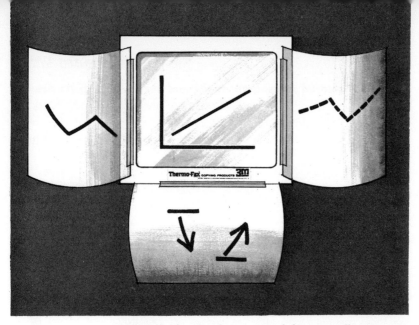

Figure 1.15. Overlay is one of the most effective ways to teach with overhead projection. This illustration shows you a typical overlay presentation, consisting of a basic transparency mounted in a frame and three overlays hinged to the side of the frame so they can be flipped over the basic transparency.

to prepare four separate transparencies. The first (or basic) transparency would be the boundary outline of the state. The first overlay transparency would have lines representing the rivers of the state. The second overlay transparency would depict only the mountain ranges. The third overlay transparency would show only the major cities. In preparing the transparencies, you might want to represent each component by a different color—for example, black for the boundary, blue for the rivers, green for the mountains, and red for the cities. This is possible by using grease pencil or pressure sensitive tape.

With the four transparencies prepared, you then take the basic transparency, the one depicting the boundary, and mount it into a transparency mounting frame. The first overlay transparency, the one showing the rivers, is then taped to the mounting frame so that when it is flipped over the basic transparency, the lines representing the rivers fall where the rivers of the state are actually located. Thus, the first overlay transparency is mounted in proper *registration* to the basic transparency. The second and third overlay transparencies are mounted in the same manner.

17

In using the technique in the classroom, the basic transparency and the overlay transparencies taped to it are laid on the projection stage. The overlay transparencies are flipped back out of the way, so that when the projector is turned on only the boundary lines of the state are projected and seen by the students. The subject material relative to the boundary is discussed. When the discussion turns to the rivers, you flip the first overlay transparency over the basic transparency, and the class sees the rivers in relationship to the state's boundary lines. The other two overlays are emplaced in turn, over the material previously presented as the discussion warrants.

When you complete the lesson, all overlay transparencies have been flipped over the basic transparency so that the class can see the boundary outline, rivers, mountains, and cities all in relation to each other. Once an overlay transparency has been flipped into position, it does not have to be removed from that position to present another overlay unless you so desire.

Placing the Projector for Maximum Effectiveness

Placement of the projector in the proper manner in relation to the audience is as important to effective employment as the above mentioned techniques. Whether you are standing before an auditorium filled with hundreds of students or addressing a small class, you want to make sure that *everyone* sees all of the projected image—and sees it clearly. You do this by planning for proper projector placement, keeping the following points in mind:

1. Project at an angle. With the projector angled, it's possible for you to remain in front of the class while allowing every student in that class to view the unobstructed screen (Figure 1.16).
2. Keep the position of the screen as high from the floor as possible.

Those who employ projection must also be aware of keystoning, which is the distortion pattern of projected light on the screen that can be introduced should the screen not be squared with the projector. For example, if the top of the screen is farther away from the projector than the bottom, the light pattern will be wider at the top than at the bottom.

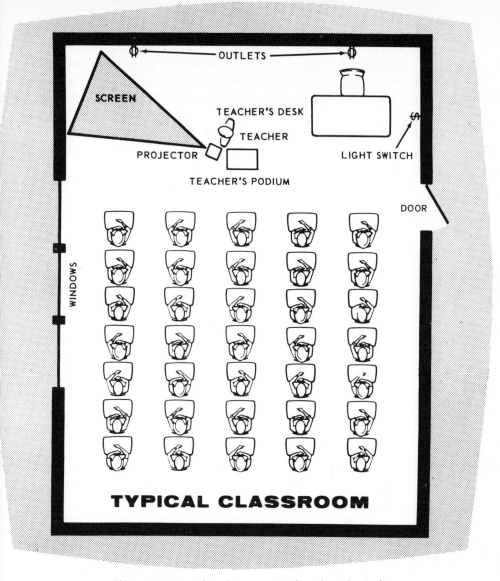

Figure 1.16. This diagram typifies the ideal classroom placement of the overhead projector vis-a-vis the class.

This occurs because the pattern of light increases in size with increasing distance from the projector.

Overcoming keystoning is a simple matter if the screen can be moved. It involves moving the screen and projector to make certain they are square with each other (Figure 1.17).

However, if the screen is permanently installed and cannot be moved, it is important that a line drawn from the projector lens to the center of the screen strike the screen at an angle of 90 degrees or, in other words, perpendicular. This would involve installing the screen at a slant, as seen in Figure 1.16.

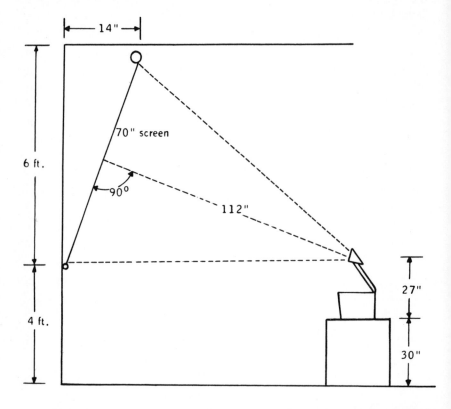

Figure 1.17. To overcome keystoning with a permanently installed screen, the screen should be placed so projected light hits it as shown. This will square up the image on the screen and prevent distortion.

Minimum Maintenance Required
By the Teacher

The only part of the system which concerns you, from a mechanical standpoint, is the small but highly powerful bulb. This bulb has a life expectancy of about 75 hours. To keep it in top condition, try not to bump or jar the projector, since the thin bulb filament can become damaged. To remove the bulb for replacement, simply grab hold of it and flip it from its spring-loaded socket. Always make sure, though, that the projector has been allowed to cool off before touching the bulb, since the bulb builds up heat during operation. It is a good idea to keep a spare bulb on hand in the event that the one in the projector burns out during a class presentation.

As regards maintenance, avoid placing your hands and fingers on glass parts. If the stage or head lens becomes dirty or dusty, wipe it off with a soft lint-free cloth dampened in a lukewarm water solution containing a mild liquid detergent.

Aside from cleaning the glass and replacing the bulb, no other part of the overhead projector, for that matter, no part of the copying machine is of concern to you from a repair standpoint. If the projector or copying machine should malfunction, a qualified service person, preferably one employed by the company that manufactured the equipment, should be called.

2.

The Transparency —
Versatility Personified

Held in the hand, an unexposed sheet of transparency film doesn't appear impressive and certainly doesn't give any indication of its potential as a teaching tool. Yet, this piece of material, which is slightly shorter than a sheet of standard typing paper, provides the teacher with an in-class visual aids capability unsurpassed by any other visual communications medium except, perhaps, closed circuit television. Added to this is the fact that transparencies are the most economical means of reproduction for visual presentation (Figure 2.1).

There are several different types of transparency materials available to meet overhead projection needs. Each type is characterized by simplicity in preparing the finished transparency, and by an amazing degree of flexibility and versatility. This chapter deals only with the types and properties of these transparency materials. Chapter 3 and all chapters thereafter will detail, by actual case studies, how you can prepare and use transparencies to further foster learning of subject matter.

Working with Transparency Materials

Transparency materials are free from shelf-life limitation, and are not affected by moisture or light (either before or after exposure). They are easily stored in a file cabinet, desk drawer, or briefcase.

The following are the general types of transparency materials available for your use in the classroom:

• **Direct reading image positive film.** This type of transparency material produces a black or frosted image, depending on the type you

RELATIVE COSTS OF PREPARING TRANSPARENCIES

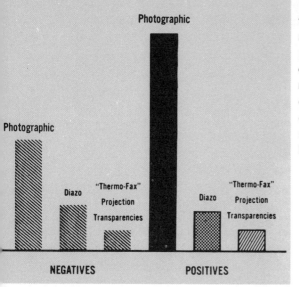

Photographic

Photographic

Diazo

"Thermo-Fax" Projection Transparencies

Diazo

"Thermo-Fax" Projection Transparencies

NEGATIVES

POSITIVES

Figure 2.1. This shows the comparative cost of making negative and positive transparencies as opposed to making reproductions for visual communication by the other two most popular means. It was computed by the 3M Company.

Figure 2.2. This is a positive transparency. It was made from an original and is an exact duplicate of that original, image-wise. The image is black while the background is clear.

Figure 2.3. This is another form of positive reproduction. However, instead of the image being reproduced as black, the composition of the transparency material enables it to be reproduced as frosted (or silver).

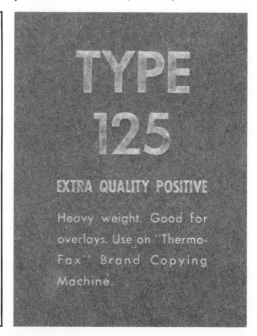

TYPE 127

DIRECT READING POSITIVE

Easy to read on or off stage. Use on "Thermo-Fax" Brand Copying Machine.

TYPE 125

EXTRA QUALITY POSITIVE

Heavy weight. Good for overlays. Use on "Thermo-Fax" Brand Copying Machine.

select, on a clear background (Figures 2.2 & 2.3). It is a positive medium that reproduces the image from a typed, printed, or hand-written piece of original material in the exact manner in which the image appears on the original, or as a frosted image on a clear back-ground. Frosted image transparencies can be interspersed in a lesson with other types to give the presentation a change of pace.

If desired, you can effect a colored image on a positive transparency by initially exposing the film to the original in the copying machine to produce an image lighter in tone than that normally needed for black-image projection. After exposure, simply trace over the lightened image area with a coloring material, such as colored pencils (Pencil Pac or Venus 200), grease pencils, or felt markers of the desired color.

Direct reading image positive film is also available with color-tinted backgrounds of red, blue, green, and yellow. These provide a black image on a subtly tinted background. You can, if you wish, outline the black image as explained above, although the color of the film back-ground is usually sufficient for obtaining the desired attractive effect.

• **Color negative films.** These negative transparency films produce a reversal of the image as seen on the original (Fig. 2.4). Suppose you have an original with a black image area and wish to make a nega-tive transparency. When the original is placed in contact with this film and exposure is made in a copying machine, the resultant image

Figure 2.4. This is an example of a negative transparency reproduc-tion in which the image is reproduced as clear, while the background becomes an opaque color.

TYPE
128

COLOR NEGATIVE

Fast, attractive color. Avail-able in Red, Green, Blue, Yellow, and Silver. Use on "Thermo-Fax" Brand Copying Machine.

on the transparency will be clear or colored, which is a negative of the image as seen on the original copy. Negative transparency materials are available that provide a red, green, blue, yellow, and silver image.

• **Color lift films.** As mentioned in Chapter 1, this type of film is used to transfer color from an original to a transparent film. However, it can only be used effectively when the color has been applied to the original by a lithographic printing process on a clay-coated paper, a method by which the ink does not permeate the paper but rests on the smooth clay coating. Most of the better known and higher quality magazines, such as *Life, Look, Saturday Evening Post* and *Better Homes and Gardens*, are printed on this type of paper. Ink can be lifted from this surface and transferred *in toto* to the color lift film for projection in full color. Only one color lift transparency can be made from any one original because the original is destroyed during the transfer process. The color lift is a heat bonding process best accomplished through the use of an infrared copying machine. However, other sources of pressure heat can be used, including a warm pressing iron, enabling at-home preparation.

Keep in mind though, that the same colored page from a magazine can be reproduced onto positive or negative transparency material by exposing the original to the transparency material in a white-light copying machine. The result, of course, is not a colored image, but one in black or white, depending upon whether you use a positive or negative film.

To use the color lift material, you must first determine if the picture you desire to reproduce is printed on clay-coated paper. This is easily done by moistening a finger and rubbing a small area in the corner of the magazine page. If a white deposit rubs off on your finger, the paper is clay-coated and you can lift any colored picture on that page onto the color lift transparency material to make a full color transparency.

• **Adhesive-backed coloring films.** These materials are not actually *films* in the same meaning as we have been using the word. You cannot reproduce an image on them. They are, instead, sheets of transparent colored materials that can be cut to any shape and adhered to a positive or negative transparency to provide a background for emphasis of image highlights. They have an adhesive back and readily stick to other transparency materials.

Suppose, for example, you make a transparency of a frog's circulatory system for viewing by a class in biology and wish to emphasize the heart and lungs. Select an adhesive-backed coloring film in whatever color you desire, cut it to shape, and simply paste it over the heart and lungs. When the transparency is projected, the class will see the circulatory system in black, let's say, but with the heart and lungs highlighted in the color or colors corresponding to the colors of the adhesive-backed transparent film you selected.

Adhesive-backed coloring films are available in red, green, blue, and yellow.

Mounting Transparencies for More Dramatic Presentation

There are many ways to mount transparencies for presentation. The commonly used ones are discussed in this chapter. No doubt, there are other ways, not mentioned in this book, which can be employed, since mounting transparencies, as does making them, leaves much to the imagination of the teacher.

There are two inherent characteristics of overhead projectors that permit you to employ practically any mounting technique you desire for dramatization of presentation. These are: (1) the large, open stage of the projector; (2) the projector's optical system which permits stacking several transparencies one upon the other, without destroying the high image resolution and clarity when they are projected.

Almost any opaque material, such as cardboard, heavyweight paper, and even file folders, can be used to mount transparencies. A basic mounting frame is made by simply cutting out a section in the middle of the opaque material to accommodate the transparency, and then fastening the transparency to the frame. To prevent light leaks which could be distracting to a class, make sure the borders of the frame cover the entire stage of the projector.

There are also ready-made mounting frames that can be purchased. These are available in various sizes and weights. Their external dimensions allow storage of transparencies in a file cabinet or briefcase.

The easiest way to attach a transparency to the frame is with self-adhering tape, such as plastic or masking tape. For simple mounting, tape all four edges of the transparency to the *underside* of the frame. Use of the underside surface of the frame for taping results in a neater mounting job and insures that the transparency will lie perfectly flat during projection. The border of the frame can be used for notations and/or identification of the transparency.

• **Mounting overlays.** The technique of mounting is perhaps best illustrated when mounting overlays (for a discussion of overlays, see Chapter 1). Overlays are usually hinged to the sides of the mounting frame, so they can be swung into position when the presentation is on the projector stage. That is, *each overlay is hinged to one border of the frame.* If you have four overlays, one is hinged to the right border, one is hinged to the top border, one is hinged to the left border, and one is hinged to the bottom border. You can then flip each overlay into position in whatever sequence you desire.

However, there is another way to mount overlay transparencies. For example, suppose you want your overlays to be swung into place in a *given* sequence to illustrate subject matter that cannot be presented in any other manner except this given sequence. All transparencies can be hinged to one border of the frame in this correct sequence. As the lesson progresses, you simply flip each overlay into place as the need arises, much the same as you would flip the pages of this book. Each of these types of mountings will become readily apparent and is illustrated throughout the remainder of this book.

It is also possible to roll mount transparencies and present them in a fixed sequence, much the same as a motion picture. However, this method was used primarily with early overhead projectors, since a roll of film was the only convenient method available for preparation of transparencies. The method is, at best, antiquated.

Roll mounting of transparencies entailed taping each transparency together in a proper sequence with transparent tape, and rolling the presentation on to a core. This was placed onto the projector by means of adapters that permitted unrolling of the material across the projector stage for viewing in sequence. Aside from the objection already noted, there were others: roll transparencies which had adhesive-backed letters or other adhesive materials applied to them caused the transparencies to stick together; there was often considerable smudging and tearing of the transparent material; the teacher lost the advantage of being able to switch back and forth from transparency to transparency for reference and review; and preparation of a roll presentation was quite difficult and time-consuming for the teacher.

Designing Your Transparencies
for Effective Communication

The design (or layout) of transparencies is as important as the actual physical act of making and mounting them. The human eye can see only so much at one time, and the human brain can comprehend and retain only a certain amount of information at any one time. For these reasons, you should keep in mind the basic elements of effective transparency design: namely, *simplicity* and *image size*.

• **Attaining simplicity.** The most dramatic transparencies are those which are simple in makeup. A transparency should illustrate one—and *only* one—point. If it contains too much information or too many details that have only secondary value to the point of a lesson, that transparency will tend to confuse the class and detract from the presentation.

The preceding sentence actually points to the two elements which you should avoid in making transparencies: (1) too much primary information and (2) information of secondary value. It is important to recognize and avoid each.

1. *Too much primary information.* Admittedly, any one lesson during a 40 minute or one hour class period can emphasize several important (or primary) points. As a teacher, you know that each point is presented and discussed individually, and the class is made to understand each point before proceeding to the next.

This basic principle of education is also a basic principle in transparency design and presentation. In a first lesson dealing with the internal combustion engine, you wouldn't tell the class the relation of pistons to valves without first discussing the functioning of the pistons and valves. Neither should you design only one transparency to show the relation of pistons and valves, and then use the same transparency when discussing the functioning of parts. Instead, you might want to prepare three transparencies, each showing the one, individual point you're going to make during a segment of the lesson.

Another important principle to keep in mind when preparing transparencies is to avoid cramming too much text onto a transparency. It makes a transparency hard to read, the information difficult to assimilate, and the presentation dull. When possible, use illustrations instead of text, developing your oral lecture around the illustration. When the illustration is no longer needed, turn off the projector so it does not detract from the lesson. This is vitally important and should be kept constantly in mind. *A transparency that's projected on the screen when it is not needed competes for student attention with the teacher's attempt to teach.*

When text is needed on a transparency, limit it to essential information. The ideal copy presentation is one with only 3 or 4 words on a transparency. However, it has been established that a maximum of 10 lines of text with each line possessing no more than 6 or 7 words can be retained by the average student.

2. *Information of secondary value.* Only transparencies which help to clarify the meaning of your comments and help the class to understand that meaning should be used. A visual aid should be used to *support* a point. It should never attempt to explain the point and thus act as a substitute for the teacher. Neither should it contain information that has no bearing upon the point being made, other than that which helps to dramatize the point.

• **Determining image size.** Lettering on a transparency should be large enough to be read easily by students in the last row. The smallest image seen on the screen must have a height of one inch for every 30 feet of viewing distance. The width and "weight" of the image must also be compatible with image height.

An Introduction to the Remainder of This Book

Chapters 1 and 2 of this book have discussed many principles, theories, and practices of overhead projection. Assuredly, much more can be said; so much, in fact, that we could fill the rest of the pages of this book with theoretical exposition. However, since illustration is the bulwark of education, we leave principles, theories, and practices at this point and turn to case studies from which, the author is sure, you will derive more benefit.

One point needs clarification before proceeding. The material in the chapters to follow is broken down into use of overhead projection in various cases of subject matter. This is done primarily for the sake of organization and ease of comprehension. The author urges you to examine everything.

You might be a teacher of language arts and can derive much information concerning overhead projection from chapters dealing with this area of education. However, keep in mind that the techniques of overhead projection, as used by teachers and discussed in this book, are studies in imagination. There is little doubt that a language arts teacher, for example, can employ, with variation, the techniques used by a mathematics teacher, a science teacher, or a vocational guidance teacher. This same principle applies to any teacher, no matter what his or her area of education.

For this reason, let us again stress this point: *Look at all techniques with a critical eye and with an eye toward using the same technique in your classroom.* There is no limit on imagination. Thus, there is no limitation on how you can use transparencies and overhead projection to communicate effectively with your class.

3.

Use of the Overhead Projector
in the Teaching of Science

Just as science is opening new vistas for mankind, overhead projection is opening new doors for teaching of science. Probably no other area of education permits the teacher to employ more imaginative projection techniques in his classroom than does science.

Consider just one source of scientific material which you can give to your students by means of projection: magazines of a scientific nature to which students are not generally exposed. Such publications as *Scientific American, Nature and Science,* and *Science* are excellent sources of current scientific data, and each student can now be introduced to these splendid publications through the medium of projection. Other magazines of a consumer nature also offer articles and reference sources that are of immense value to students—publications such as *National Geographic, Life, Newsweek,* and *Time.*

There are still other sources of scientific, mathematical, and other information which students will find invaluable in the learning process and which can be presented via projection—pamphlets and booklets prepared and distributed by governmental and private industrial research groups; textbooks and workbooks written for and about science; the actual equipment used in experiments; your own notes and sketches; even a student's homework paper and, certainly, the results of an experiment performed by him as part of an assignment or on his own initiative.

Projector Converts to "Lab"

Science, of course, is a discipline that demands experimentation as much as it demands theories and principles laid down in a book. Your

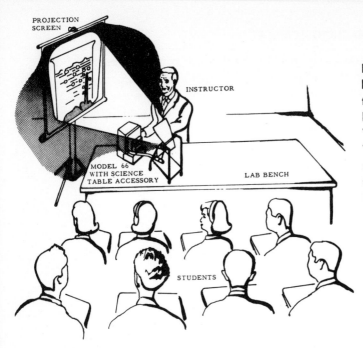

PROJECTION SCREEN

INSTRUCTOR

MODEL 66 WITH SCIENCE TABLE ACCESSORY

LAB BENCH

STUDENTS

Figure 3.1. The overhead projector is quickly turned into a science laboratory by use of the Vertical Stage Science Table. It permits experiments conducted by the teacher or a class member to be viewed by all.

Figure 3.2. Overhead projection permits class viewing of an experiment in process.

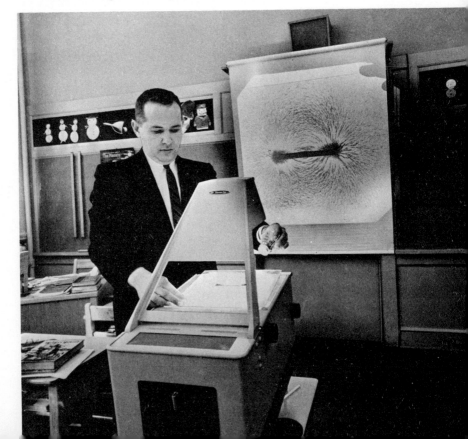

everyday overhead projector is quickly transformed into a "scientific laboratory" that permits vertical positioning of experiments and presentation of them on a 10 × 10 inch projector stage. Practically every Alyea T. O. P. S. experiment—for example, titration, manipulation, electrolysis, and meter readings—is readily projected onto the screen from the front of a fully lighted classroom for all to see. Transparent materials appear in full color, opaque materials appear as silhouettes.

This is all done by means of the Vertical Stage Science Projector, which is adapted for use with your regular overhead projector, as seen in Figure 3.1. The image is positioned on the screen by pivoting the science table mirror and projector head.

The science table is not the only way in which you can use overhead projection to conduct experiments. The flat projector stage itself forms an excellent "laboratory." For example, suppose you wish to demonstrate the principles of magnetism. All you need is a clear glass plate, a magnet, and a tumbler of iron filings. The glass plate is placed over the projector stage, the magnet is placed on top of it and the iron filings are sprinkled. (Naturally, the projector should be turned on.) The entire magnetic process is projected, and the students can see the filings scamper as they are drawn into the magnetic field (Figure 3.2).

The examples outlined below demonstrate how the medium of overhead projection can be used and expanded to meet the needs of the teacher in educating youngsters in science. Note particularly that even the most complex areas of study can be transformed into simple transparencies for projection. This has a decided psychological effect of making the most complex scientific study appear simple to the student.

Furthermore, one should never overlook, especially in the elementary grades, the interrelating of cross disciplines. For example, mathematics, English, spelling, and economics can be crossed with science via overhead projection. This goal should be strived for by the teacher and she, in turn, should encourage the introduction of cross disciplines into her classroom by student participation.

Study Thermometer Relations Via Projection

In physical science classes at Luther Burbank Senior High School in Sacramento, California, the relationships and differences between Fahrenheit, Centigrade and absolute Kelvin thermometers and readings are taught by means of nomographs. Materials used include nomographs showing the relationships and differences between each of the three thermometers, sheets of direct reading image positive transparency film, and grease pencils or felt markers of different colors.

The sketch and transparency film are placed into contact with each other and run through an infrared or white light copying machine. If an infrared machine is used, it takes just four seconds to make the transparency.

The transparency is placed on the stage of the overhead projector and, at the appropriate time in the lecture, is projected onto the screen to demonstrate the differences between Fahrenheit, Centigrade, and absolute Kelvin thermometers and temperatures (Figure 3.3). If desired, each of the three can be colored differently with coloring pencils or felt markers, or outlined directly on the transparency with adhesive-backed coloring films.

If overhead projection were not employed, the teacher would have had to prepare 100 copies of the diagram by a reproduction process (ditto, Diazo, etc.) for the 100 pupils taking the course. Or she would have had to draw the sketch of the three types of thermometers on a chalkboard, which would have taken considerably longer than four seconds.

At the same school, projection is used in a biology class numbering some 130 students to test their knowledge of the structure of the human heart. Used are a nomograph of the human heart with numbered areas for identification by the students and a sheet of direct reading image positive transparency film.

The sketch and transparency film are run through the reproduction machine to make one transparency. The transparency is placed on the stage of the projector and the image is projected for the duration of the test (Figure 3.4). Students are instructed to number a sheet of blank paper, so that the numbers on their papers correspond to the numbers shown on the image being projected. Then, they are told to name the parts of the heart as seen on the projected image.

This was done for all classes in the course with just one transparency. If overhead projection were not employed, the teacher would have had to prepare 130 copies of the worksheet by another reproduction process.

Language and Principles Taught Concurrently

In another biology class, this one at North Hunterdon Regional High School in Annandale, New Jersey, students are taught the language and

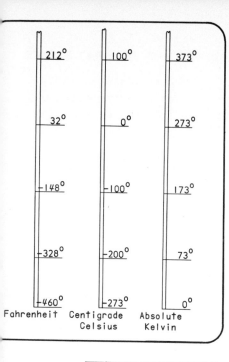

212°	100°	373°
32°	0°	273°
-148°	-100°	173°
-328°	-200°	73°
-460°	-273°	0°
Fahrenheit	Centigrade Celsius	Absolute Kelvin

Figure 3.3. What better way to show the differences between thermometer scales than by having them displayed side-by-side. Overhead projection makes this possible.

Figure 3.4. The overhead projector can be used for giving a test. Reproducing this image by a reproduction process other than the transparency method would have taken the teacher considerable time, as would drawing the sketch on a chalkboard. And, of course, not every teacher can draw.

HUMAN HEART - WORKSHEET

#
NAME _____
Biology _____
Date _____
Sci. 337.3 (1:1) 12/64

INSTRUCTIONS: In the spaces provided below place the correct names of the structures numbered on the diagram.

1. _____   6. _____   11. _____
2. _____   7. _____   12. _____
3. _____   8. _____   13. _____
4. _____   9. _____   14. _____
5. _____   10. _____   15. _____

Sci. 337.3 (1:1) 12/64

principles of frog dissection *at the same time* via projection. In outlining his purpose in using the method, the teacher has emphasized the following:

> The beginning student of biology must learn a new vocabulary if he is to understand the simplest essentials of the life science. We feel that to teach biology one must teach basic principles. However, before these principles can be taught the student must learn the language of biology. *With the use of the overhead projector, we can teach both language and the principles at the same time.* We also know that the student learns more quickly and retains more information if he uses his eyes and ears simultaneously.

The materials he uses are a nomograph of a frog, a sheet of clear direct reading image positive transparency film, and colored grease pencils.

The nomograph of the frog and a sheet of positive transparency film are run through the reproduction machine to make the transparency. The transparency image is projected onto the screen.

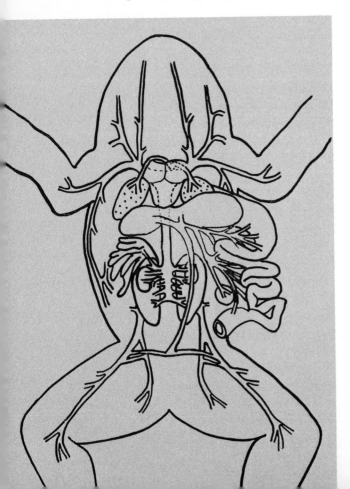

Figure 3.5. Seeing while doing aids students in learning. Frog dissection is one area in which overhead projection helps to simplify procedure and enables familiarization with terms.

As the dissection by students takes place, the teacher points, at appropriate times during the lesson, to various body parts shown on the projection. He colors that part of the transparency and explains its function. The students see the part *in* the frog as they perform the dissection; they have a reference point to go by because of the projected image; and they are able to take notes from the teacher's lecture as they proceed through dissection (Figure 3.5).

The following is an extract from the lesson showing how the lecture can be coupled with the transparency and dissection:

> The *posterior vena cava* (color in red as you talk) collects blood from the liver (color in brown) via the hepatic veins (color in blue) and from the kidneys (color in green) via the renal veins (color in yellow) . . . . .

Projection and Earth Science

Teaching primary grade students what causes night and day has assumed a new approach in earth science classes at Ramona Elementary School No. 79 in Jacksonville, Florida. In outlining the objectives, a teacher made the following point concerning the teaching of this scientific discipline to students in the lower grades.

> Many of these concepts have been impossible for the primary children to grasp, but we believe with the use of well-drawn transparencies they are brought within a realm of more understanding of them.

Materials used include diagrams and photographs showing the shadowed side of the earth in relation to the sun to illustrate day and night, and transparency films (either negative or positive) to reproduce diagrams and photographs.

Two concepts are stressed in the lesson: (1) the sun lights our solar system; (2) rotation of the sun brings absence of light and, hence, night. The transparencies bring home forcefully these concepts to the young pupils. To determine the effectiveness of the lesson, the teacher has the pupils make their own drawings of how we get night and day. These are made into transparencies and projected (Figure 3.6). The children, of course, are enthusiastic about doing their work in anticipation of having it shown to their classmates by means of overhead projection.

In chemistry classes at Mercyhurst College in Erie, Pennsylvania, the hybrid orbitals of carbon are demonstrated by projection. A sketch

This is Day.

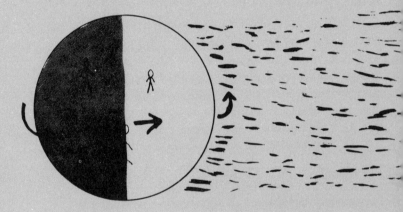

This is Night

You have day and night because the earth turns.

Figure 3.6. This is a young pupil's image of day and night after only one lesson in the difficult-to-grasp earth science in which overhead projection was used. The drawing was made into a transparency and projected for the whole class to see, as were drawings of the other pupils. The teacher injects even more interest in the lesson by letting pupils make their own transparencies and operate the overhead projector.

showing the hybrid orbitals of carbon, sheets of transparent film, colored grease pencils, and strips of red and yellow transparent tapes are used.

After the basic transparency is prepared, the presentation is made even more dramatic by adding color. A strip of red transparency tape is used to emphasize the heading: "Hybridization of Atomic Orbitals." Strips of yellow transparency tape are used to emphasize the "Four sp³ Hybrid Orbitals of Carbon." Colored grease pencils are used as follows to color in the center of each atomic orbital on the prepared transparency: red to color the 2s orbital; yellow to color the 2 px, 2 py, and 2 pz orbitals; blue to color in the four sp³ orbitals; and black to color in the geometric pattern.

This pattern transparency is one of the many used by Mercyhurst's Chemistry Department to portray complex structures by three-dimensional drawing (Figure 3.7). These permit the entire class to view the models and allow for student use for review or original development.

Seed Germination Vividly Portrayed
by Projector

Plant science is taught to first and second grade pupils in the Healy Elementary School in Detroit, Michigan. One aspect of the course is to

Figure 3.7. Overhead projection lends itself ideally to the teaching of chemistry concepts. Here, color is used to add emphasis to the lesson, as well as for purposes of derivation.

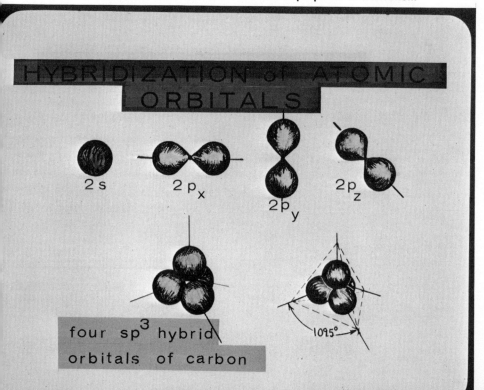

teach the corresponding growth of both root and stem systems in germinating seeds.

Four sketches are used as follows: (1) seed; (2) rootlet; (3) sprouting shoot and growing root system; (4) growing stem and foliage, and spreading root system. Four sheets of clear direct reading image positive film to reproduce each of the four sketches are employed. Colored grease pencils or felt markers are used to add a dramatic effect.

Each of the four sketches is reproduced as a separate transparency. The transparency showing the seed is colored as follows: the seed is colored yellow and the area around it is colored brown to portray the ground. The rootlet shown in the second transparency is colored brown. The growing root system of the third transparency is colored brown and the sprouting shoot is colored green. The spreading root system of the fourth transparency is colored brown and the growing stem and foliage is colored green.

In making the sketches, each of those showing shoot and root were lined up in proper registration on the first sketch showing the seed. Thus, when one of the transparencies showing root and/or shoot is placed over the basic transparency showing the seed, the shoot and/or root falls exactly into position with respect to the seed.

The four transparencies are used in overlay fashion. The basic transparency, the one showing the seed, is taped into a mounting frame. The other three are hinged to the sides of the mounting frame, one to each side.

In use, the teacher discusses the seed and shows a transparency of it (all other transparencies are hinged back, so they are not projected [Figure 3.8a]). The teacher then explains that a rootlet comes from the seed. She flips the overlay transparency showing the rootlet over the basic transparency so the pupils can see the growth in relation to the seed (Figure 3.8b).

The teacher then explains that the rootlet begins to grow into a root system and a shoot eventually sprouts from the seed. The overlay showing the rootlet is flipped back from over the basic transparency, and the second overlay showing the sprouting shoot and growing root system is flipped into position (Figure 3.8c).

Finally, the teacher explains how the stem and foliage grow and protrude through the ground, while the root system spreads. The overlay showing the sprouting shoot and growing root system is flipped back out

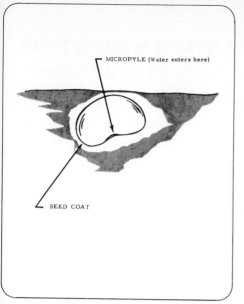

MICROPYLE (Water enters here)

SEED COAT

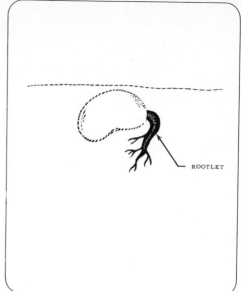

ROOTLET

Figure 3.8a. This sketch forms the basic transparency in the teaching of how a seed germinates. The seed image on the transparency is colored yellow, and the area around it is colored brown. This basic transparency is kept in position and projected at all times during the lecture.

Figure 3.8b. This is a sketch of the first overlay which is flipped over the basic transparency seen in Figure 3.8a at the appropriate time in the lecture. After discussion culminates, the transparency is flipped back out of the way.

Figure 3.8c. The second overlay, flipped into position over the basic transparency, reveals the relation of growing root system and sprouting shoot to the seed.

Figure 3.8d. This is the final overlay used in this lesson. It shows the growing stem and foliage, and the spreading root system.

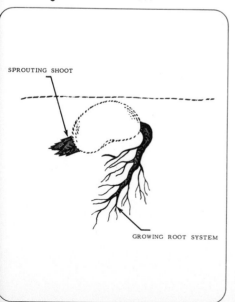

SPROUTING SHOOT

GROWING ROOT SYSTEM

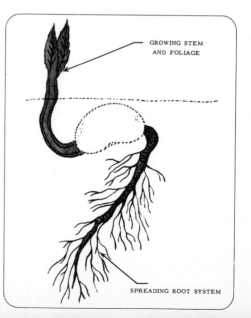

GROWING STEM AND FOLIAGE

SPREADING ROOT SYSTEM

of the way, and the third overlay transparency, the one showing the growing stem and foliage, and spreading root system, is flipped into place.

The teachers making use of the overhead projection system to teach science at the Healy Elementary School have this to say about its application:

> The overhead projector probably has more varied uses in the science room than any other room in the school. The time saved by the use of this machine can be used to do the many other things required of a teacher. It enables the science teacher to present certain scientific concepts in a manner which would be extremely difficult using any other method. By the use of basic overlay transparencies, concepts, ideas, and data may be developed in stages and proper sequence.

Weather Science Unit Presented

In weather science classes at Gledhill Street Elementary School in Sepulveda, California, upper elementary grade pupils are taught the principles of the weather map as a prelude to a more extensive study of weather. Materials employed for utilization of overhead projection include weather maps, sketches, cardboard flaps to be used over transparencies as revelation devices, clear and colored direct reading image positive films, and grease pencils.

This one lesson makes use of 10 transparencies. To a side of each transparency is hinged a worksheet referring to the information on the transparency for use by the teacher in lecturing. The transparencies, in order of presentation, show the following:

• *Transparency No. 1:* This transparency is made by reproducing a detailed weather map, obtained from the U. S. Weather Bureau, onto a sheet of transparency film by use of an infrared copying machine (Figure 3.9a). The accompanying lecture material, hinged to the side of the transparency and referred to while the image of the weather map is being projected, states the following:

> Can you read a weather map?
> A weather map tells the whole weather story by using just a few numbers and symbols. A jet pilot reads a weather map in order to be sure to follow the smoothest, fastest, and safest route. You, as a passenger, can read the weather map to learn the weather conditions of the area you are leaving, the weather below in the areas

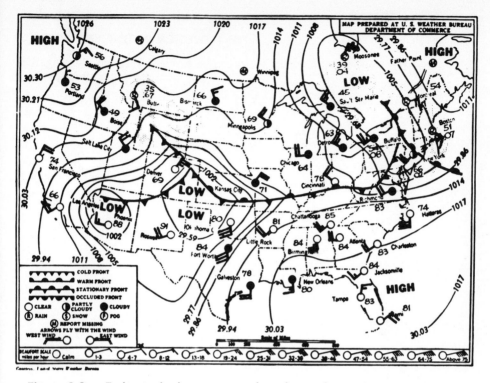

Figure 3.9a. To begin the lesson on weather, the teacher projects a transparency of a weather map, emphasizing the subject matter of the particular lesson which, in this case, is the symbol for wind. Materials for transparencies are available from many governmental and private industrial agencies. Weather maps such as this one, for example, can be obtained daily from the U.S. Weather Bureau. There is usually no charge for this material.

enroute to your destination, and finally what kind of weather to expect at your destination.

Today we are going to learn about one of the symbols on a weather map.

Wind is very important in weather forecasting, so we will begin by learning about the symbol for wind.

(*Teacher points to symbol on map and in legend.*)

On a weather map this is the symbol for wind.

(*Change to frame #2.*)

• ***Transparency No. 2:*** This transparency is made by tracing an outline map of the United States onto a plain sheet of white, opaque paper and drawing in a sketch of an airplane in the center of the map. Arrows are placed to the rear (tail-end) of the plane to portray the force of the wind behind the plane (Figure 3.9b). The accompanying text reads as follows:

Figure 3.9b. As the lesson evolves, the teacher brings in topics to foster student interest as, for example, a jet aircraft. Note the simplicity of each of these transparencies. It's wise to keep in mind this basic principle of transparency making — *one idea to a transparency.*

Figure 3.9c. This transparency shows wind direction and velocity at high altitudes. Throughout the lesson, the teacher uses the pointing technique. This is *not* done by walking to the screen and pointing to projected material. Instead, the teacher remains at the projector stage where he can have control over the material and uses an ordinary pencil or his finger to point to the desired portion of the transparency. The image of the pencil or finger is projected onto the screen.

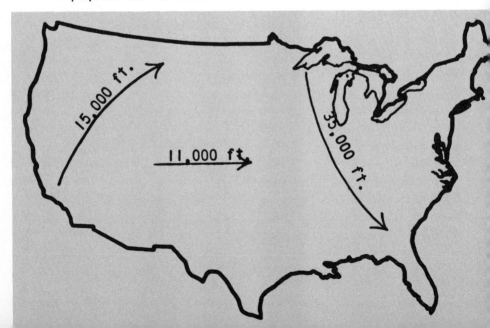

A weather map tells a flight crew and the jet pilot which route will be the shortest flight in terms of time. An airplane flying with the wind, a tail wind, goes faster.
(Teacher points to direction of wind and plane.)
(Change to frame #3.)

• **Transparency No. 3:** This transparency is the same as transparency No. 2 except that the arrows portraying the wind are heading into the nose of the plane. The accompanying text reads as follows:

An airplane flying against the wind, a headwind, flies slower.
(Point to direction of wind and plane.)
(Change to frame #4)

• **Transparency No. 4:** This transparency is again an outline sketch of the map of the United States. Superimposed on the map are three sweeping arrows going in different directions to portray wind direction. Written over each arrow are numerals to signify altitude of the wind current (Figure 3.9c). The accompanying text states the following:

Wind direction varies at different altitudes, so the captain of the flight must decide not only the best route, but the best altitude.
(Point to direction arrows and altitudes.)
For example, at 11,000 feet, there may be a west wind at the same time that there is a south wind at 15,000 feet and a north wind at 35,000 feet.
A wind traveling toward the east is called a west wind because it comes from the west.
(Point to west wind.)
A wind traveling in a northern direction is called a south wind because it comes from the south.
(Point to south wind.)
Likewise, a wind traveling in a southern direction is called a north wind because it comes from the north.
(Point to north wind.)
(Change to frame #5.)

• **Transparency No. 5:** This transparency is made by first sketching, on a sheet of white opaque paper four wind symbols to signify four different wind directions and velocities. The original is then reproduced onto a sheet of clear-colored direct reading image positive transparency film. Two strips of black, plastic tape, running horizontally and vertically, are used to divide the transparency into the four parts. The teacher then cuts out four cardboard rectangles to cover each of the four parts of the transparency and tapes them to the sides of the transparency mount in their respective positions (Figure 3.9d). A grease pencil is used by the teacher in presenting the lecture material relative to the transparency, as follows:

(Open trap #1.)

The symbol for wind looks like a queerly shaped arrow. Instead of an arrow with a point, it has a circle. *(Point)* One side of the tail feather is missing. *(Point)* This one symbol tells us three important things about the weather in different parts of the country —or the world. It tells us the direction of the wind. *(Point)* The circle is the point of the arrow. This arrow points east. It shows that wind is blowing from west to east. *(Point)* It is a west wind traveling toward the east.

(Open trap #2.)

Can you tell in which direction this symbol shows that the wind is blowing? Yes, it is blowing west. It is an east wind.

The second important fact these symbols tell us is the speed of the wind. The length of the lines and the number of lines on the tail of an arrow tell us how many miles per hour the wind is moving.

(Point to trap #1.)

This symbol indicates the speed to be 1 to 3 miles per hour.
(With grease pencil write 1-3 beneath the symbol.)
(Point to trap #2.)

This longer line on the tail of the arrow shows that the speed of the wind is 4 to 7 miles per hours.

(With grease pencil, write 4-7 beneath the symbol.)

(Open trap #3.)

Notice that to show wind speed of 8 to 12 miles an hour, another line has been added. Is it as long as the line to the left? *(Point)*

(With grease pencil, write 8-12 beneath the symbol.)

Let us look at this symbol. It indicates a wind from 25 to 31 miles an hour. Notice the number of lines and the length of the lines on this symbol.

(With grease pencil write 25-31 beneath the symbol.)

The teacher now removes frame #5 from the overhead projector, and as a prelude to frame #6, which she places on the projector but doesn't reveal, she says,

The third fact that the arrow shows is the condition of the sky.

• **Transparency No. 6:** This transparency is prepared in the same manner as transparency No. 5, but now the teacher introduces a new element to dramatize the lesson—*color*. Various wind symbols, each

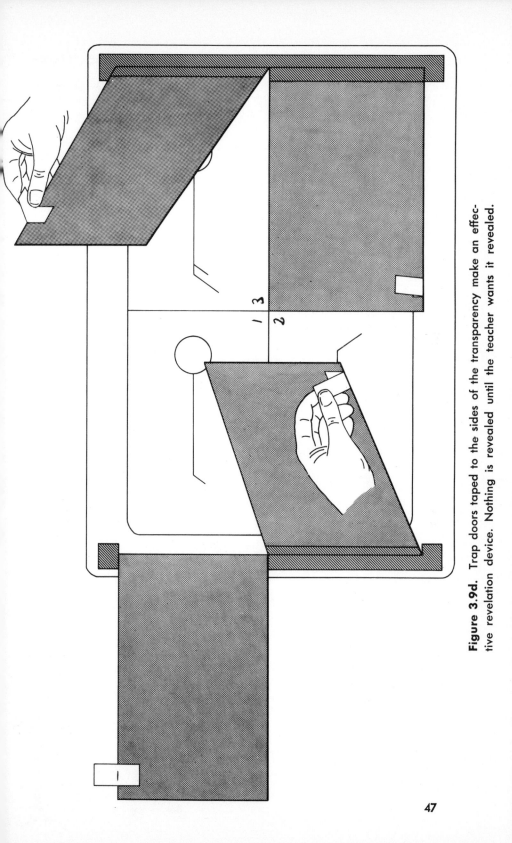

Figure 3.9d. Trap doors taped to the sides of the transparency make an effective revelation device. Nothing is revealed until the teacher wants it revealed.

showing something different, are sketched onto white, opaque paper. Each one, though, is reproduced on a different colored direct reading image positive film. The colors used are red, blue, yellow, and green. When the transparencies are reproduced, each is trimmed to the same size and placed into a mounting frame. Strips of plastic tape running vertically and horizontally across the transparencies hold them firmly in place. Again, trap doors are used to cover the transparencies and make revelation possible. The text accompanying this frame is as follows:

(Open trap #1.)

The letters and the shading within the circles tells us the sky condition of the areas on the weather map.

(Point) An "R" in the circle means rain. Can you tell in which direction the wind is blowing *(Point)* and at what speed it is blowing? *(Point)* Yes, it is blowing toward the east and the wind speed is between 25 to 31 miles per hour.

(Open trap #2.)

An "S" in the circle means snow. Can you tell in which direction the wind is blowing? *(Point)* Do you remember the speed of wind this line on the tail shows?

(Open trap #3)

A half-shaded circle means partly cloudy. Can you guess what a fully shaded circle means?

(Open trap #4)

Yes, it indicates an area that is completely overcast.

Figure 3.9e. The introduction of cartooning into a lesson increases pupil interest. This cartoon shows the effect of a 1 to 3 mile per hour wind, with the symbol for this velocity wind clearly shown on the transparency so pupils can relate.

The teacher now removes frame #6 from the projector and places #7 on stage, keeping it closed until she introduces it with the following:

Do you have any idea of what a wind of 1 to 3 miles an hour looks like?

• **Transparency No. 7:** This transparency is a cartoon type drawing on a sheet of white, opaque paper. The drawing shows a girl pointing to the sky, a house in the background with smoke coming lazily from the chimney and a tree standing upright. On top of the drawing is the wind symbol for a 1-3 mile an hour wind (Figure 3.9e). The text reads as follows:

(*Point to Symbol.*)
The day would look like this. The air would feel calm and quiet.

The teacher removes the transparency from the projector stage and places frame #8 on the stage. Before revealing it, she introduces the subject with the following comment (the white paper covering the transparency masks the image from the screen):

Do you know what a wind of 8-12 miles an hour would look like?

• **Transparency No. 8:** This transparency shows the same picture as transparency No. 7, except that the smoke from the chimney and the tree are drawn to symbolize a gustier wind. Text for the transparency is as follows:

(*Point to symbol.*)
This picture illustrates a wind speed of 8 to 12 miles an hour. Can you notice the movement of the air?

• **Transparency No. 9:** The transparency, again, is similar to the previous two, except that the characters are shown to portray a very gusty wind. The girl in the cartoon is seen trying to hold an umbrella from being blown away (Figure 3.9f). Lecturing material for this transparency is as follows:

(*Point to symbol.*)
A wind of 25 to 31 miles an hour would do this to your umbrella.

At this point, the projector is turned off and the teacher passes out maps of the United States to the children. She quizzes them on their understanding of the information revealed during the lesson. At the end of the quiz, she places a transparency of the map possessing the correct symbols on the projector and turns it on (Figure 3.9g). This is transparency No. 10, and the teacher states the following:

Figure 3.9f. This transparency, following two others showing less gusty wind velocities, vividly indicates to the pupils the effect of a 25 to 31 mile per hour wind.

Figure 3.9g. After a quiz, the teacher uses the overhead projector so the students can determine if their answers are correct.

Your map should look like this. Check each symbol carefully. If you have made any mistakes, be sure you find out why.

In preparing this interesting lesson on weather, the teacher has used techniques which are only possible through the use of overhead projection. These are revelation, and the introduction of color to liven up the lecture. Other techniques employed were pointing and the chalkboard technique (the grease pencil acting as the chalk and the transparency as the chalkboard).

Overhead projection permitted this teacher to cover more material in less time and in a more dramatic and inspiring way.

Physiology and Entomology Lend Themselves to Projection

Physiology students at Warren G. Harding Senior High School in Warren, Ohio, are acquainted in one lesson with the small intestine. The relation of the artery and vein configuration and direction is emphasized. To make this difficult information understandable, overhead projection is used. Materials employed with the projector are a cross-section drawing of the villus (small intestine), sheets of clear direct reading image positive transparency film, and red and blue felt pens.

On the prepared transparency, the artery portion is colored red, and the vein portion is colored blue (Figure 3.10). This same transparency is also used for classes in biology and health.

Entomology has always fascinated the student. This fascination is now heightened because of projection, as witnessed in sixth grade classes at Northbrook Elementary School in Southfield, Michigan. In this particular example, the body parts of ants and the function of each part are the areas of study.

Materials employed with the projector are a drawing of an ant, individual drawings of each part with text to explain the function of the part, and sheets of transparency film (clear and/or colored).

The transparencies are made and introduced at appropriate times during the lesson. Without the use of the projected images, which are seen clearly by all the class, the lesson would be less than effective. According to the instructor who prepared the lecture –

Very often an illustration, page, or diagram is found that could have meaningful results if shown to the entire class. One's choice

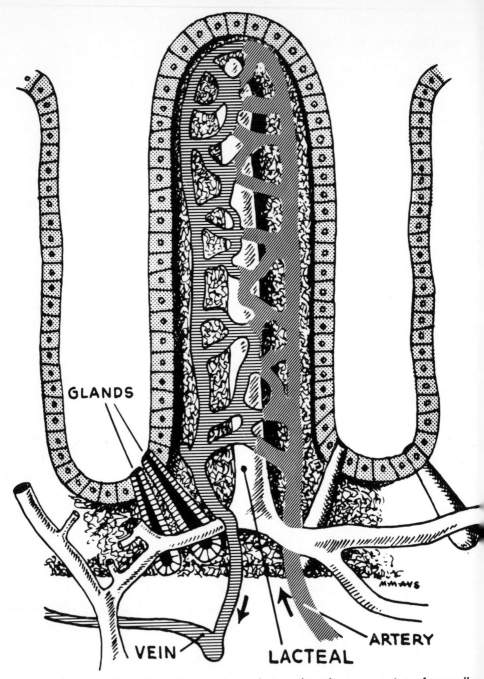

GLANDS

VEIN   LACTEAL   ARTERY

Figure 3.10. What better way to show a class the cross-section of a small intestine than to project it on a screen. This same principle is effective in microscopic work. Slides are set up for the pupils to look at, but before the experiment begins the teacher projects an image of what the students will see. This projection and explanatory notes by the teacher permit the students to orient themselves before looking into a microscope.

as a teacher is limited to holding the picture up for all to see, which is a failure because it:

1. Wastes time showing it to all sections of the room.
2. Picture is too small for anyone to see any detail.
3. While turning back to one side of the room, you lose part of the class.

Figure 3.11. All teachers are faced with the problem of showing information such as this to a class. Holding the picture up doesn't solve the problem, because not all can see it. Passing it around or walking around with it wastes class time. Projection can solve the problem.

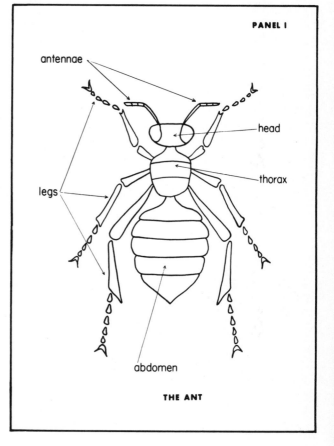

The overhead and its uses of transparencies enable the teacher to face the class and have everyone see the picture at the same time, without any loss of control (Figure 3.11).

4.

Use of the Overhead Projector
in the Teaching of Mathematics

There is no longer a conventional way to teach mathematics. This exacting science is changing from year to year, and the mathematics teacher must adapt his methodology to these changes.

The development in the student of computational skills is no longer important. Machines make computations much faster and much more accurately than man. Philosophically, then, the role of the mathematics teacher in the modern classroom is to develop in his students the ability to understand, manipulate, and create mathematical concepts and systems.

To bridge the gap between the traditional and advanced modern approaches to mathematics, the teacher must provide simple, clear, and concise explanations of unfamiliar terms and principles. In teaching mathematics from the standpoint of today's concepts and tomorrow's needs, therefore, the teacher should have available any tool that makes explanation of reasons and of terms absolutely clear to the student. The overhead projector is such a tool.

Advantages to the
Mathematics Teacher

Enumerating every specific application of the overhead projector in the mathematics classroom is, at best, an impossible task. This chapter does contain several applicable methods from which you can obtain a firmer understanding of the remarkable versatility of this tool. Generally, though, the overhead projection system offers the mathematics teacher the following advantages, as it does the teacher of other areas of learning:

• The teacher must always keep uppermost in his mind the psychology of learning mathematics—that is, the way in which the students' minds work to grasp fundamentals and theories. Thus, a tool that permits organized sequential development of mathematical principles is invaluable. No other tool proves to be such a valuable asset as does the overhead projector.

• With so much to be taught in any one class, time cannot be wasted. Teaching tools must be examined critically with an eye to selecting only those which conserve the time and energy of both the teacher and the student. The traditional chalkboard tool holds few advantages when compared to the modern overhead projector in achieving this goal of time and energy conservation. With the overhead projector, the teacher has at his fingertips as much material as he can possibly use to develop concepts and theories. There is no space problem, and there is no longer danger of a lesson being accidentally erased by someone who doesn't see the "SAVE" warning sign scrawled in a corner. Furthermore, with an overhead projector a teacher can always repeat a segment of a lesson without losing valuable time in erasing and rewriting. Thus, attention does not waver and enthusiasm does not wane.

• The mathematics teacher strives to keep a balance in a lesson between development of skills and development of understanding. Only a tool as versatile as the overhead projector enables one to do this by means of varying presentations, drills, and quizzes. Furthermore, materials are always close at hand for use as often as required in referring the student back to something already presented. Since mathematics is a developmental science, with one theory hinging on the understanding of the previous theory, reviews of this nature are frequently required.

Assuredly, then, the overhead projector is an everyday tool for the mathematics teacher, not something to be dragged into the classroom only on occasion. To broaden your understanding and tease your imagination of how overhead projection can be used in your classroom in the teaching of mathematics, we present the following case histories enumerating what your contemporaries in the field have already done.

Overhead Projection
Outlines the Rules

There are "Rules We Go By" in mathematics. Such was the title of an effective transparency presentation developed at the Westview Ele-

Figure 4.1a. This attractive title page, transformed into a transparency, introduces a lesson in mathematical rules to primary grade pupils. Needless to say it caught their interest immediately.

mentary School in Chattanooga, Tennessee (Figure 4.1a). The presentation consists of four transparencies and a title transparency that clearly depicts rules of addition, subtraction, multiplication, and division and, equally important, the relationship and similarities of these rules to the mathematical processes. The presentation enhances the development of basic mathematical skills.

Although simple in makeup, each of the transparencies imparts the respective rule in an attractive style with an impact on the student not possible by use of other teaching tools. Animation and text are effectively combined.

After making the originals on white opaque paper, the teacher reproduces the material on sheets of direct reading image positive film. Color that strengthens the presentation is then added to the transparencies by use of crayon, felt marker, or other coloring devices.

As you can see, each transparency contains two rules to show the relationship of the rule to respective mathematical processes. The first transparency, for example, contains the rules: "If zero is added to a number, the answer is that number," and "If zero is subtracted from a number, the answer is that number." (Figure 4.1b). The other trans-

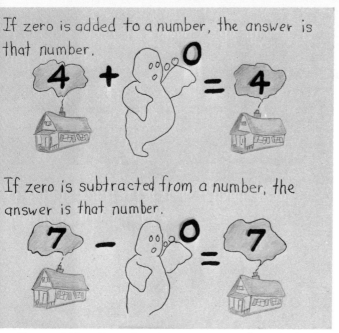

Figure 4.1b. Here the ghost gives a mathematical rule.

parencies show the relationships and similarities of rules in addition and multiplication (Figures 4.1c and 4.1d), and multiplication and division (Figure 4.1e).

Figure 4.1c. Note how the teacher changes the animated characters from transparency to transparency to maintain interest and expectation.

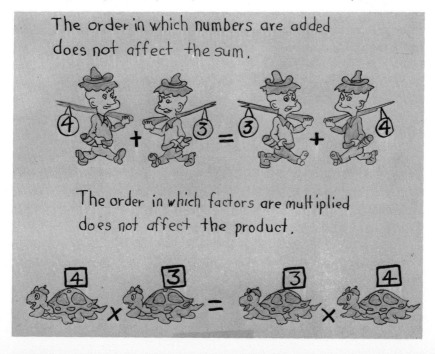

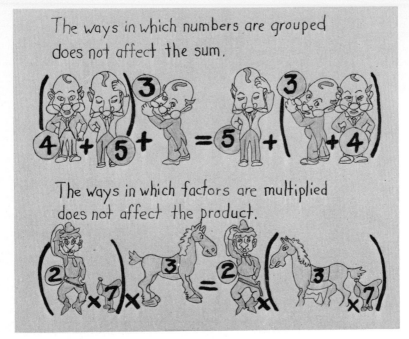

Figure 4.1d. Color is added to the transparencies after the black original is reproduced onto the film.

Figure 4.1e. Being practically indestructible, transparencies such as this can be used year in and year out.

Teaching Fractions
with Overhead Projection

Another effective technique was developed at Westview Elementary to teach a basic concept of fractions. The technique utilized an overlay scheme which has the following as its parts:

• *Basic transparency*, consisting of a large square that fills the area with text reading "Whole or One" (Figure 4.2). This transparency is mounted and is projected continually during the presentation of the overlays.

• *Overlay #1*, consisting of a square divided equally by a vertical line. Each of the divisions is marked "½" and text outside the square reveals that ½ plus ½ equals 2/2 and that 2/2 equals 1 (Figure 4.2). This overlay is hinged to the side of the basic transparency. When flipped into

Figure 4.2. This illustration shows one way to use an overlay transparency technique to teach pupils fractional mathematics.

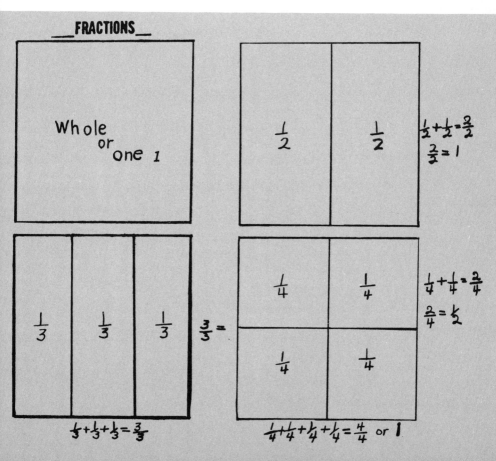

position, the lines of the square of overlay #1 coincide perfectly with the lines of the square projected from the basic transparency. They are, then, in registration, and the students are able to observe visually that ½ plus ½ does, in fact, equal 1.

• **Overlay #2,** consisting of a square divided equally into three equal parts (Figure 4.2). This is hinged to the other side of the basic transparency and reveals to the students that ⅓ plus ⅓ plus ⅓ equals 1. The students now know this for a fact because *they can see it for themselves.*

• **Overlay #3,** hinged to the top of the basic transparency, consisting of a square divided into four equal parts. Thus, the student is able to see that ¼ plus ¼ plus ¼ plus ¼ equals 1 (Figure 4.2).

The basic concept exemplified by this easily employed overhead projection technique makes learning of fractional principles clearly understandable to even the slowest learner. There are few other, if any, teaching tools that permit this type of teaching methodology.

An Alternate Method of Teaching Fractions

Another method of fractional mathematics teaching is employed in fourth grade classes at the Edward R. Johnstone Elementary School in Vineland, New Jersey. The method is, in reality, a quiz type in which the teacher utilizes class members to broaden student interest, as well as to establish in her own mind whether principles have been grasped.

The lesson concerns itself, in this case, with division of objects into thirds. After introduction and discussion of principles, the students are asked to draw pictures portraying each of the principles just explained —that is, ⅓ of 12, ⅓ of 6, ⅓ of 9, and ⅓ of 15 (Figure 4.3). As many of these drawings as time permits are then projected by the teacher for all to see.

According to the teacher who developed the technique, "It broadens understanding by allowing the class to visualize thirds of a variety of objects. They (the students) can also judge the accuracy of the principle and spot errors." Class discussion is naturally enhanced.

Overhead Projection in High School Math

When students enter high school and are introduced to such mathe-

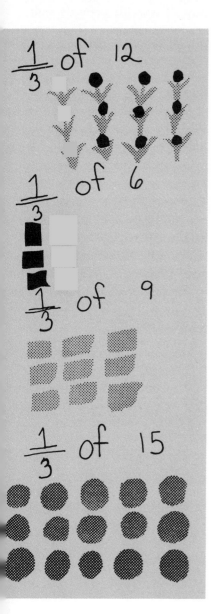

$\frac{1}{3}$ of 12

$\frac{1}{3}$ of 6

$\frac{1}{3}$ of 9

$\frac{1}{3}$ of 15

Figure 4.3. Students made drawings to determine their knowledge of fractional principles. Each is transformed into transparency form for projection.

matical principles as the horizontal and vertical parabola, irrational co-ordinates, the quadratic function, and concurrent lines, the maze often becomes an impasse. Traditionally, high school math teachers have taken the approach that repetition is the best form of learning, and they pound away at principle after principle, trying to embed into the student's mind words which he can repeat like a parrot on a Friday quiz.

Modern mathematics leaves no room for such parroting, and neither does it leave much room for this long followed technique. The student must learn the *why* of a principle, so he can apply that principle to the *how* aspect of modern mathematics.

There is no mathematical theory or principle that cannot be made clearly understandable to students, as math teachers at Fall Branch High School in Fall Franch, Tennessee, demonstrate for us. Through the use of overhead projection, complex mathematics becomes a living, breathing science which puts the slower mathematics pupil on an almost equal par with the gifted math student.

One lesson at Fall Branch, for example, has as its objective the teaching of angular terms. Just what is meant by a reflex angle, an obtuse angle, and an acute angle? Words spoken by the teacher could prob-

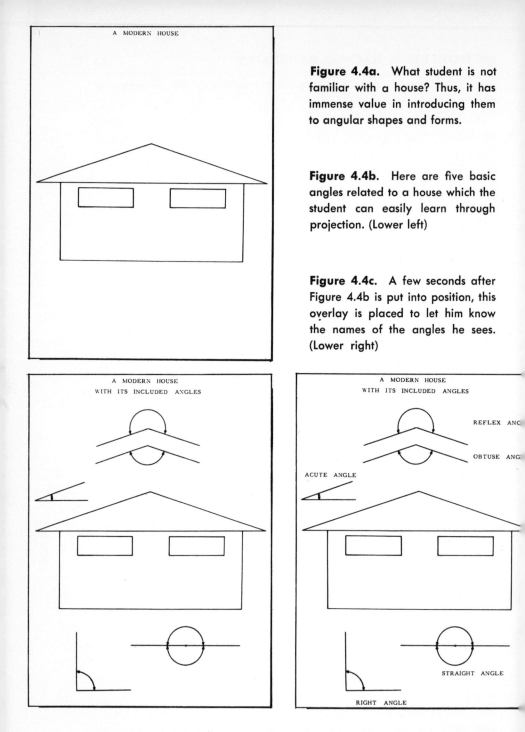

Figure 4.4a. What student is not familiar with a house? Thus, it has immense value in introducing them to angular shapes and forms.

Figure 4.4b. Here are five basic angles related to a house which the student can easily learn through projection. (Lower left)

Figure 4.4c. A few seconds after Figure 4.4b is put into position, this overlay is placed to let him know the names of the angles he sees. (Lower right)

ably relate the information so all will understand—*in time.* By using overhead projection to demonstrate angles and by relating them to something with which all students are familiar, this time is saved and students are better able to gain greater insight into the meanings of angular terms.

The familiar object selected is a house, simply drawn on a piece of white opaque paper and reproduced onto a sheet of direct reading image positive film (Figure 4.4a). The transparency is mounted and forms the basis for an overlay approach to the problem.

The first overlay hinged to the basic transparency depicts five angles formed in the construction of the house (Figure 4.4b). Two angles are placed near where the roof of the house peaks. Another angle is placed alongside the eave of the roof. A fourth angle is formed where the side of the house meets the foundation. And the fifth angle is drawn close to the straight line of the foundation.

As the students observe these angles and relate them to the angles of the house, a second overlay is dropped into place on top of the other two. This transparency gives the names of the angles, so the student is able to see at a glance which term relates to which angular shape. As you can see in Figure 4.4c, the angles formed by the roof are spelled out as the reflex angle and the obtuse angle. The angle formed at the eave is termed the acute angle. The angle formed by the house's siding and foundation is shown to the student as the right angle. And the straight line of the foundation is termed the straight angle.

Question: How long does it take you to explain the meanings of these terms to your students so they understand them? The above lesson is covered in a matter of minutes.

Student Participation Is Enhanced By Projection

Student participation is an essential ingredient in the teaching of mathematics. At Fall Branch, participation is imaginatively coupled with overhead projection to teach the students the complex process of locating points having irrational coordinates.

Basis of the method is a transparent circle made on color *negative* film. The original is first drawn on opaque white paper and then reproduced onto the negative film. Thus, all black lines on the original are reproduced as clear on the transparency, and the white background of the original is reproduced as black (opaque) on the transparency. The clear portion of the transparency is the part seen when projected. After the transparency is made, the circle is cut out (Figure 4.5).

Another transparency is made of a sheet of graph paper, but this one is reproduced onto direct reading image *positive* film.

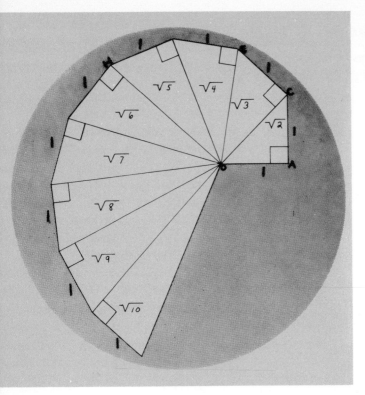

Figure 4.5. This device coupled with a transparency reproduction of a sheet of graph paper is used to teach location of square roots using Pythagorean relations.

Figure 4.6. This device supports the teacher's explanation of the complex algebraic numbering system.

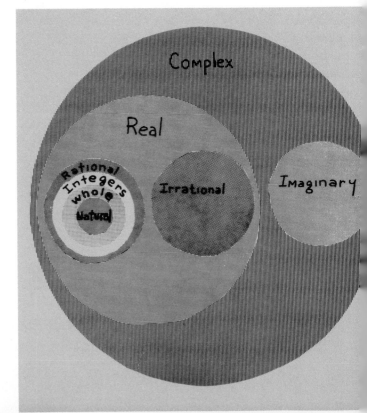

The aim of the lesson is, of course, to locate the square root of any number line by using Pythagorean relations.

With the transparencies placed in position on the projector stage (transparency of the graph paper on the stage, with the negative transparency of the circle lying on top), students are called to the projector to go through the procedure. Students remaining in their seats are quick to take part, catching errors and making suggestions. All calculating work is done by the student with a crayon pencil right on the transparency graph. Lines on the transparency can be erased easily, and the transparency reused.

The complex number system used in algebra often finds the student staring into space, a blank expression on his face. Students in Algebra II at Fall Branch no longer stare blankly. They are experiencing something new—quick understanding through graphic presentation.

Several transparent circles of varying sizes are made on direct reading image positive film of different colors. They are then cut out and titled. Finally, they are integrated by taping them together with transparent tape and projected to support the teacher's explanation of algebraic numbering (Figure 4.6).

According to the teacher who developed the methods, "By using color-cued circles, the student can visualize the relationship of one number to the entire complex number system. He sees that the complex contains real and imaginary numbers. In the group of real numbers, he finds both rational and irrational numbers. Within the group of rational numbers, he finds integers; within integers, whole numbers; and within whole numbers, natural numbers."

Geometric theory is also made vividly understandable through the use of overhead projection at Fall Branch. Again, the overlay comes into play, but in a different and imaginative manner.

"Take the theorem that the bisectors of the angles are concurrent in a point equidistant from the sides, and prove it, John," the teacher says as he lays a transparency of a triangle on the projector (Figure 4.7).

John approaches the projector and takes a sheet of clear, *unexposed* transparency film from the rack. He places it over and tapes it to the transparency already on the projector. He takes a red crayon pencil and transparent ruler, and demonstrates that the intersection of the angle bisectors (point 0) of the triangle are equidistant from the sides of the triangle.

Leaving the other two transparencies in position, he takes another sheet of clear, unexposed positive transparency material and places it over and tapes it to the other two transparencies. With a compass equipped with a crayon pencil adjusted properly, he further demonstrates that point 0 is in the center of the triangle.

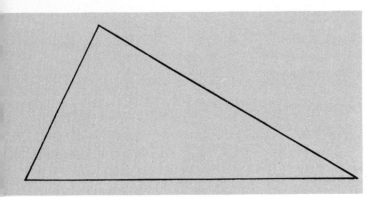

Figure 4.7. A simple transparency such as this forms an excellent basis from which students can learn geometric theorems.

Question: Can this be done as effectively on a chalkboard while the chalk flies hither and yon as it snaps from a chalkboard compass, and while the chalk makes squeaky sounds as John presses too hard? Furthermore, if you have to go back in the lesson to review a point, isn't it easier simply to remove one of the transparencies than to erase and rewrite.

Overhead Projection Eliminates Lengthy Description

Until they began using overhead projection, mathematics teachers at St. Mary's School in Mt. Morris, Michigan, found it difficult to portray for their students the essence of geometric theorems. Introduction of complicated figures in the classroom to relate visual credence to verbal fact was not usually possible, since the time lapse between class periods was too short to allow drawing of the multi-lined figures on the chalkboard. So, the teacher struggled on, trying to draw pictures with words, and the students struggled along, trying to visualize mentally what had been said.

Enter overhead projection! Now, the teacher can prepare complex drawings in advance. Once prepared, the transparencies can be used year after year since they do not deteriorate. Figures 4.8 and 4.9 depict

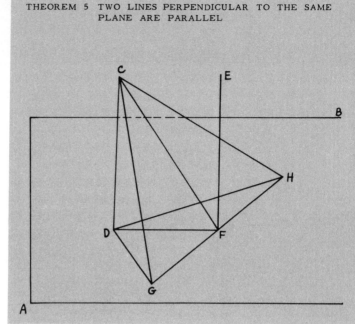

THEOREM 5 TWO LINES PERPENDICULAR TO THE SAME
PLANE ARE PARALLEL

Figure 4.8. A diagram such as this one, although simply drawn, is usually impossible to get on a chalkboard in the short time between class periods. Preparation the night before and reproduction onto a sheet of transparency film make introduction of the drawing into the classroom possible. Once the transparency is made, it never has to be remade, but can be used continually.

THEOREM 8 THE SECTION OF A CIRCULAR CONE MADE BY
A PLANE PARALLEL TO THE BASE IS A CIRCLE

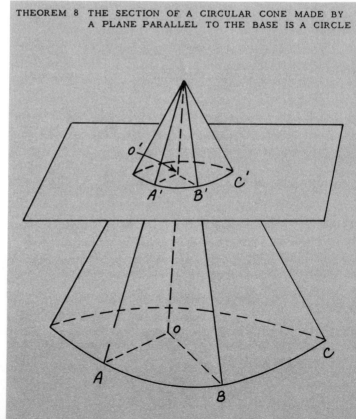

Figure 4.9. Drawings such as this, used in a class in geometry, eliminates the student's age-old cry, "I don't see how!"

two of these complicated drawings. Figure 4.8 is used to prove the theorem that two lines perpendicular to the same plane are parallel. Figure 4.9 is used to explain that the section of a circular cone made by a plane parallel to the base is a circle. Can you draw these two on your chalkboard in the 10 minutes allocated to you between class periods? Not usually!

No longer is there groping in St. Mary's geometry classes for descriptive words, and no longer do pupils have to draw pictures in their minds.

Overhead Projection Makes Traditional Math Teaching Passe

"In the traditional treatment of mathematics," teachers at Howard W. Bishop Junior High School in Gainsville, Florida contend, "the student was taught a collection of miscellaneous tricks and meaningless juggling of symbols. It is the purpose of our mathematics department to present mathematics in such a way that the reasons for different mathematical processes become evident. To achieve this end, it is necessary to be concerned with mathematical structures—that is, with a systematic derivation of mathematical processes from a few assumptions. The emphasis on structure conforms with current opinion concerning the improvement of the mathematics curriculum.

"In order to attain this goal," they continue, "we use extensively the overhead projector along with a series of locally produced transparencies to cover all phases of the mathematics curriculum at all grade levels. To illustrate the projected use of transparencies we offer one of the more difficult exercises in which various mathematical processes can be demonstrated. We try to illustrate a problem with graphical solutions so a student can more easily visualize these processes as they appear in various problem situations."

The problem offered by the teachers is an algebraic one concerned with mixtures of the type used by chemists which, as you know, cause considerable trouble for even the best of students. The simple original transparencies are prepared by the teacher beforehand.

The first group of originals is prepared in overlay form (Figures 4.10a, 4.10b, 4.10c and 4.10d). Generally, the problem is to reveal graphically what takes place when a solution is decreased or increased in concentration, and what takes place when the volume is changed or must not be changed so students can work such problems algebraically.

The use of the first group of transparencies progresses as follows.

1. Begin by projecting the basic transparency (Figure 4.10a), showing the problem and the original container.

2. Put the first overlay into place over the basic transparency (Figure 4.10b), showing what must be done before anything can be added.

3. Place the second overlay into position atop the other two (Figure 4.10c), showing what is added to replace the solution removed.

4. Project the final overlay, placed on top of all the others, to show the final concentration, emphasizing that the volume is still equal to that in the original container (Figure 4.10d).

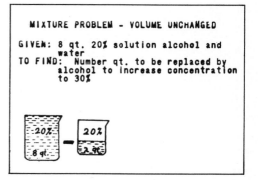

Figure 4.10a. This is the basic transparency used to teach pupils in algebra the mathematical processes employed in determining chemical solutions.

Figure 4.10b. The first overlay is superimposed over the basic one (Figure 4.10a).

Figure 4.10c. The problem progresses with the introduction of the second overlay on top of the other two (Figures 4.10a and 4.10b).

Figure 4.10d. The problem is completed with the placement of the final overlay.

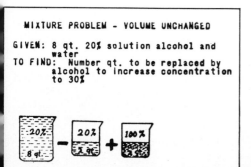

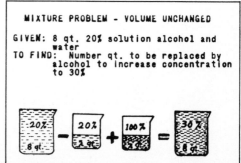

```
(a) In terms of amount of alcohol:
    Let x = number qts solution replaced
          by alcohol
    .20(8) - .20(x) + 1.00(x) = .30(8)
      1.6 - .2x + x = 2.4
             .8x = .8
               x = 1 Qt alcohol
```

```
(a) In terms of amount of alcohol:
    Let x = number qts solution replaced
          by alcohol
    .20(8) - .20(x) + 1.00(x) = .30(8)
      1.6 - .2x + x = 2.4
             .8x = .8
               x = 1 Qt alcohol


(b) In terms of amount of water:
    Let x = number qts solution replaced
          by alcohol

    .80(8) - .80(x) + 0(x) = .70(8)
       6.4 - .8x = 5.6
              .8 = .8x
               x = 1 Qt alcohol
```

Figure 4.11a. The first transparency shows in algebraic terms how to solve the problem posed in Figures 4.10a to 4.10d in terms of the amount of alcohol.

Figure 4.11b. The overlay is flipped over the one seen in Figure 4.11a to show an alternate method of solution. Immediately, the student can see that whatever method he uses to solve the problem, the answer is the same.

At this point in the lesson, and with the first group of transparencies still on the projector to be used for reference, there is a discussion of the two possible mathematical ways the problem may be solved. When the discussion has spent itself, the first group of transparencies is removed from the projector stage. The next group of transparencies, again tied together in overlay form, is introduced (Figures 4.11a and 4.11b), and the problem progresses.

5. Project the first transparency (Figure 4.11a), showing the algebraic equation written in terms of the amount of alcohol.

6. Project the overlay transparency (Figure 4.11b) showing the alternate equation written in terms of the amount of water.

The two solutions are observed one on top of the other, and the students are able to determine the evolvement of both.

Using Manipulating Devices on the Overhead Projector

The ability to project ready-made transparent mathematical tools for exercise work onto a screen has been discussed in previous chapters. Some of these devices include transparent rulers, triangles, protractors, compasses, and slide rules.

Fifth and sixth grade teachers at West Salem Elementary School in Salem, Oregon, have gone one step further. It is in these classes that youngsters are introduced to geometric shapes for the first time.

The teacher makes use of a manipulative device designed from four strips of oak tag and hinged together at four places with pin clips (Figure 4.12a). Moving the parts of the device changes its shape (Figure 4.12b). Instead of making a transparency, which would eliminate the moveable capability, the teacher simply places the device itself on the stage of the overhead projector. An opaque image is cast, and the students are able to see geometric changes taking place as the teacher manipulates the device. Transparent mathematical tools (rulers, compasses, triangles) can then be used on the projector and in relation to the manipulative device so all can see, mathematically, the changes in geometric design.

Another type of manipulative device is used at the Alice Bell Elementary School in Knoxville, Tennessee, to teach primary grade chil-

Figure 4.12a. This simply made manipulating device is used to introduce the student to geometric shapes.

Figure 4.12b. By moving the device, the teacher changes the shape. The change is readily seen by students when projected onto a screen.

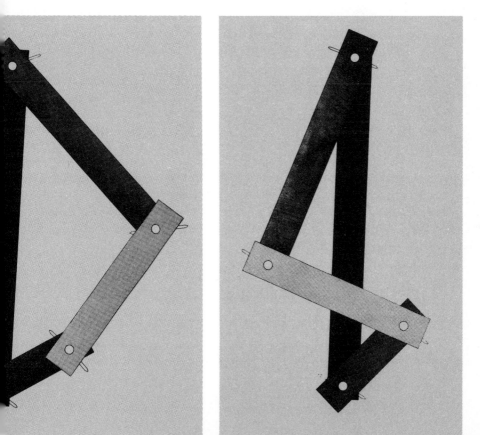

dren how to tell time. The teacher draws a simple clock, without hands, on a sheet of opaque white paper and reproduces it onto direct reading image positive film. If she desires, she adds a bit of color by outlining the clock dial in red, or whatever color is wanted.

She then makes two hands for the clock, punches a hole in the center of the transparent clock dial, and inserts the hands with a pin clip (Figure 4.13). The hands, of course, can be moved.

When placed on the projector and projected, the positive image of the clock dial and the hands of the clock can be seen as a movable opaque image. Since the hands can be moved freely by the teacher or student, the entire class is able to follow their direction and determine, in fact, how a clock works.

According to the teachers who use the device, "This method eliminates having to hold a regular clock and moving the hands at the same time. Furthermore, we know the hands of our manipulative clock will remain in place without having to hold them."

Figure 4.13. A manipulative clock is an excellent tool to use when teaching youngsters how to tell time. Since it would be too small for all students to see if held by the teacher, it is instead projected so all can see, including students in the last row.

Simplicity Is The Byword

In this chapter, the author has attempted to portray some of the more advanced and refined methods of overhead projection in the teaching of mathematics. Assuredly, there are many others, some of which haven't been devised as yet and some of which you will probably think of yourself. However, the teacher should not lose sight of the basic methods which can also be employed to great advantage and to the benefit of the student in learning the theories and principles of this exacting science.

Reproducing a page from a workbook . . . using a blank, unexposed sheet of transparent film and a grease pencil to show students the steps in problem solution . . . use of transparent tapes and graph paper reproduced on to transparent film to teach graphing . . . cutting out simple geometric shapes from opaque paper and projecting opaque images—these and many more are excellent methods that can be employed and which are readily available to any teacher.

Refined or basic, though, the mathematics teacher, as well as any other teacher using overhead projection, should keep in mind that there is no substitute for simplicity in visual projection. A cluttered projection which only tends to confuse is as useless as no projection at all. A simple projection that makes the one point to support the teacher's lecture is invaluable.

5.

Use of the Overhead Projector
in the Teaching of Reading

Although considered part of the broad program of study known as the language arts (see Chapter 6), reading is often divorced from and treated as a separate course of teaching because of its magnitude and importance. This is especially true in the elementary grades, while in the upper grades the two are usually brought together and treated as one entity.

For this reason, the subject of how the overhead projector can be used to teach reading is, in this book, treated separately. However, the reader should keep in mind that the relation of one to the other cannot be dismissed. For example, one cannot divorce today's reading lesson from yesterday's spelling lesson or from last week's grammar lesson. The advantages and necessity of basing one upon the other are readily apparent. Thus, this chapter and chapter 6 should be examined with a critical eye in an attempt to integrate the use of transparencies. For instance, there is no reason why a transparency used yesterday to teach spelling cannot be reviewed today to teach a reading lesson in which the same spelling words are employed.

Although reading is not as stimulating to the imagination as science and mathematics, but rather more stereotyped and limited, the overhead projector can be used to excellent advantage in the reading room. In possibly no other area of study is the axiom "you learn by seeing" as true as it is in reading, since reading *is* seeing. Many variations of basic projection techniques can, in fact, be employed. We deal with these now.

Applying the Concrete to Teach Reading Symbolism

The teachers at West Salem Elementary School in West Salem, Oregon, contend that "We believe 'one picture is worth a thousand words' and that the concrete is more easily understood than abstract symbolism." Based on this philosophy, these teachers instruct youngsters in reading.

"Between the ages of 7 and 10, learnings of a permanent nature take place as the result of concrete, not hypothetical experience," a primary reading teacher at West Salem claims. "Use of the overhead projector helps us to build the mental images so basic to the abstract symbolism of reading."

As examples to support this contention, the following transparencies used in the reading room at West Salem are offered:

Figure 5.1 is intended to acquaint pupils with rhyming words. The transparency is made directly from a page in a workbook simply by putting the page in contact with a sheet of direct image positive transparency material and running the two through an infrared copying machine. After the transparency is made, it is placed on a projector

Figure 5.1. The overhead projector can be used to teach rhyming words.

Figure 5.2. Association is a forerunner of reading comprehension. The overhead projector can be put to good use in this area by simply copying workbook or other material onto transparency film and projecting it.

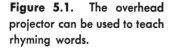

Which Rhyme?

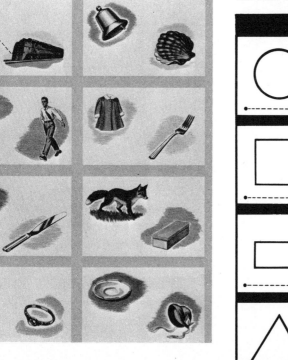

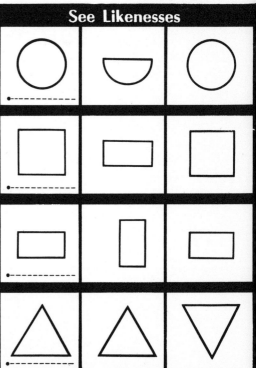

and the image cast. The students are then urged to tell which words applying to the symbols in each of the blocks are rhyming words.

Figure 5.2, which is another transparency made by copying a page directly from a workbook, is used to help children associate shapes. This is a forerunner, of course, to reading comprehension.

Figure 5.3 shows an exercise in teaching children not only the basics of reading, but also how to follow directions. It, too, is a direct reproduction of a page of a workbook onto a sheet of direct image positive transparency material. After the exercise based on the projected image is completed, the children are asked to submit their own coded messages, which the teacher lets them reproduce on transparency film and place on the projector. The fact that the children are permitted to operate this "magic" machinery adds to the interest of the class.

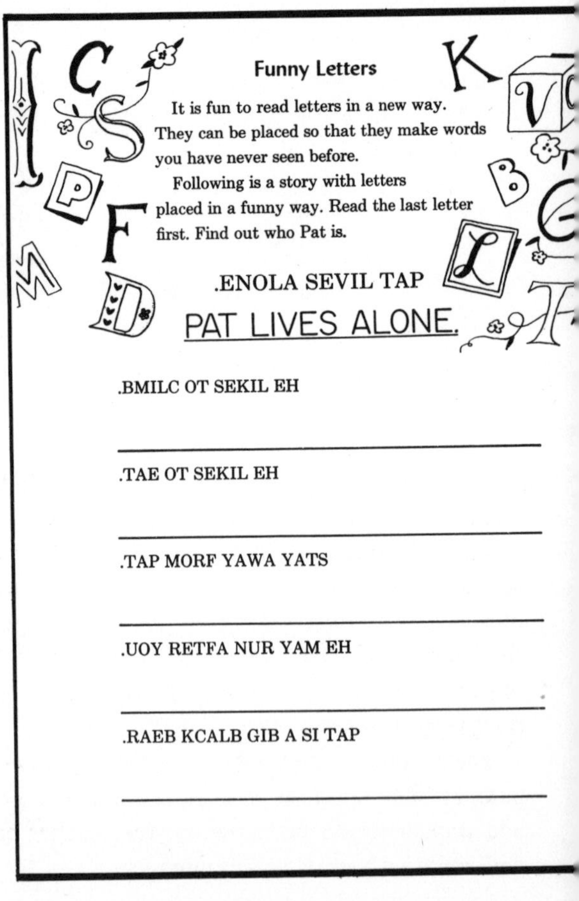

Figure 5.3. The overhead projector can be used for a dual purpose —in this case, to teach children the basics of reading and how to follow directions.

Funny Letters

It is fun to read letters in a new way. They can be placed so that they make words you have never seen before.

Following is a story with letters placed in a funny way. Read the last letter first. Find out who Pat is.

.ENOLA SEVIL TAP

PAT LIVES ALONE.

.BMILC OT SEKIL EH

.TAE OT SEKIL EH

.TAP MORF YAWA YATS

.UOY RETFA NUR YAM EH

.RAEB KCALB GIB A SI TAP

Figure 5.4. This transparency, and a series of others based on the same principle, is useful in teaching students beginning sounds.

With a child's message projected, the remainder of the group acts as a team in deciphering the message.

Transparencies are also employed at West Salem to teach beginning sounds. The teacher prepares a large drawing in the left-hand corner of a piece of opaque white paper. In the right-hand corner, she prints the capital and small letter which is the first letter of the name of the object. Then, all around she draws other objects that may or may not start with the same letter (Figure 5.4).

The opaque white paper is placed into contact with a sheet of transparency film (positive and clear) and the original is reproduced. To add impact to the presentation, the teacher colors each of the objects with coloring pencils or felt markers.

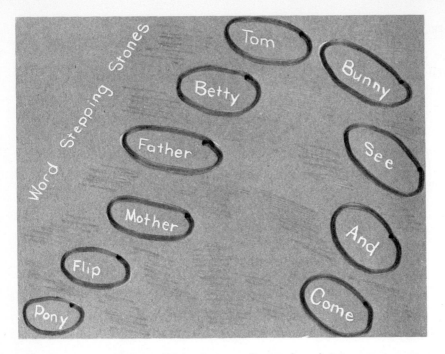

Figure 5.5. A "game" transferred into transparency form helps reading comprehension while fostering interest.

During the lesson, she points to the large drawing in the left-hand corner. To do this, she does not approach the screen on which the image is being projected, but uses the pointing technique at the projector itself. She asks the children for the name of the object, emphasizing the first letter and how it appears. She then asks them for the names of the other objects by pointing to each on the transparency, keeping the question constantly before the children as to whether the names of these objects begin with the same letter as the name of the large object. Naturally, the letter itself is continually referred to so the students can learn what the letter looks like at the same time they are learning what it sounds like.

Another technique employed in reading classes at West Salem and facilitated by overhead projection is most interesting. It's called the Stepping Stone Game.

The teacher takes a piece of clear direct image positive transparency material or, for that matter, a clear piece of acetate and writes several words on it, outlining the words with a grease pencil. Around them she scribbles blue, scrawly lines to represent water (Figure 5.5).

The object of the game is for the students to pronounce the words correctly. If a student fails to do this, he falls into the water and is out of the game.

Using Projection to Teach Homonyms

In reading classes at Maple Ridge Elementary School, Somerset, Pennsylvania, overhead projection is used in still other ways. In the teaching of homonyms, for example, the overlay technique is effectively employed.

The basic transparency contains the heading, HOMONYMS, and the first and last letters of a few words (Figure 5.6a). Note that the transparency is not cluttered, but is kept simple.

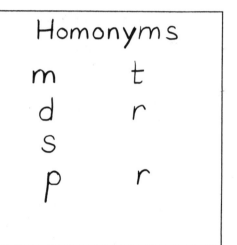

Figure 5.6a. This is the basic transparency in a lesson concerned with homonyms. Note its uncluttered appearance.

Figure 5.6b. The first overlay transparency used with the one seen in Figure 5.6a forms words when flipped into position. (Lower left)

Figure 5.6c. The second overlay transparency when used with the ones seen in Figures 5.6a and 5.6b forms the homonyms of the words. (Below)

The first overlay transparency contains, in color, the middle letters of the words (Figure 5.6b). To add to the transparency and to further increase value of the lesson, the teacher draws in a caricature of one of the words. This overlay is hinged to the side of the basic transparency.

The second overlay, which is hinged over the other two, lists in a different color the letters which make the homonym (Figure 5.6c). Again, an object is drawn that refers to one of the words, preferably an object that is the homonym of the one drawn in overlay 1.

You can, of course, see how this works. The basic transparency is projected and discussed in terms which point out to the children that two words having the same pronunciation and the same first and last letters have different meanings. The first overlay is emplaced to start the illustration.

Then, the first overlay is removed and the second overlay is placed over the basic transparency. To bring the point across even more forcefully, the second overlay is removed and the first put back into position. Then, the second overlay is placed right over the first, so the children can see for themselves how the letters change.

Another excellent device which uses overhead projection has the objective of offering for the teacher a quick way to use a basal reader in order to locate poor readers and to test students for placement into reading groups at the beginning of a term.

The teacher tells the class at the first or second session that she has something special for them to read. She projects the "story" on the screen and each student reads two to five sentences (Figure 5.7). The teacher watches for refusal, hesitation, and difficulty. The teacher can at any time switch to another transparency.

Figure 5.7. Overhead projection is used at the first lesson of a term to locate poor readers and so the teacher can determine how to break down a large group into small, homogeneous groups for reading.

One of the most interesting birds which ever lived in my bird-room was a blue-jay named Jackie. He was full of business from morning till night, scarcely ever still. He had been stolen from a nest long before he could fly, and he had been reared in a house long before he had been given to me as a pet.

Figure 5.8a. In this transparency, the illustrated leaves are colored red.

Figure 5.8b. In this transparency, the illustrated leaves are colored yellow.

Figure 5.8c. In this transparency, the illustration is a row of homes to represent a town.

Figure 5.8d. Put together, the transparencies seen in Figures 5.8a, 5.8b, and 5.8c blend to make an effective illustration that visually portrays the poem.

Using Projection for Poetry Appreciation

The overhead projector is of much value at Maple Ridge in teaching appreciation of poetry. In the first grade, for example, the transparencies seen in Figures 5.8a, 5.8b, and 5.8c are used in overlay fashion for this purpose.

First the teacher flashes the entire poem on the screen using a transparency other than the one shown. She reads it to the children. A discussion is held about the poem and about the pictures the students form in their minds from it.

Then, the poem is flashed a line at a time. The basic transparency (Figure 5.8a) contains the first line and an illustration, the color of which coincides with the words of the poetic line.

The first overlay transparency contains the second line of the poem and is hinged to the side of the basic transparency (Figure 5.8b). Again, the color of the illustration coincides with the line of poetry.

The second overlay (Figure 5.8c) contains the last line of the poem and a colored picture to illustrate that line.

The entire projection, with overlays in place, can be seen in Figure 5.8d. As you can see, they make a composite picture and complete poem for the children.

Flashing the poem line by line helps the children to memorize it. The children then recite the entire poem (the projector is turned off as they do so) and are told to draw a picture of their own that the poem suggests to them.

Using Projection to Teach Phonics

At Park Elementary School in Parkersburg, West Virginia, overhead projection is used to teach phonics. Figure 5.9 is an example of this. The teacher designs and prepares this transparency herself. It is reproduced onto a sheet of direct image transparency film by use of an infrared copying machine.

A grease pencil is placed on the stage of the projector, the transparency is put into position and projected, and students in turn are called to the projector to complete a segment of the exercise. Students in their seats watch the result on the screen and, if a child at the projector performs correctly, are told to pronounce the word. If the child at the projector gives the wrong answer, class members are asked to correct him. Grease pencil lines are easily erased after and during the lesson.

An excellent technique to prepare children for reading was developed by teachers at St. Mary's School in Mt. Morris, Michigan, by simply reproducing a page from a workbook onto a sheet of clear direct image positive transparent film and coloring in certain parts with colored

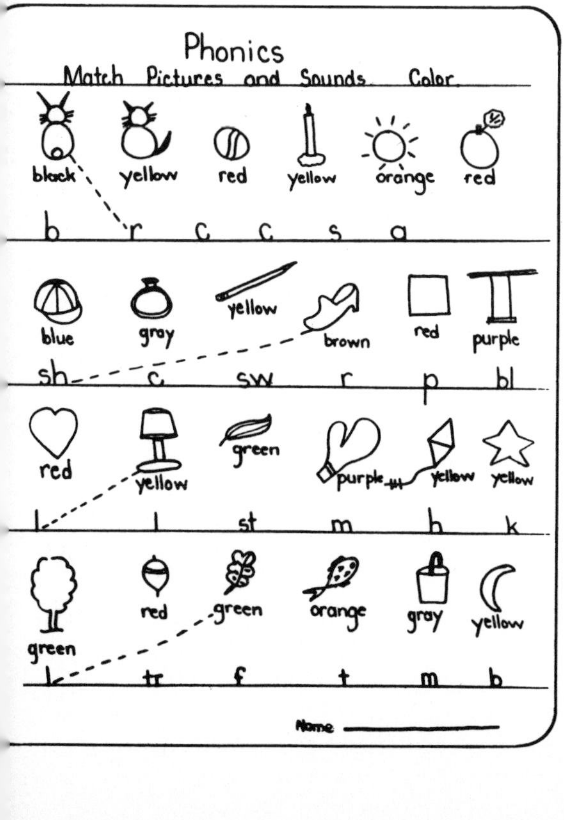

Figure 5.9. This transparency is an example of how overhead projection can be used to teach phonics. The idea behind it is to use the transparency as a chalkboard so students can physically participate in the lesson.

pencils. In the illustrations seen in Figure 5.10, the line going from the rabbit to the first carrot is colored and the line going from the second carrot to the third is colored. All carrots are colored.

Figure 5.10. Transparencies and overhead projection are used to solve the problem of left to right eye movement for youngsters first learning to read.

The object of the exercise is to get children to develop left to right eye movement in readiness for reading. As you know, educators have discovered that many children fail to learn to read, simply because they have difficulty in developing left to right eye movement. As the teacher demonstrates this movement by pointing to the "path" the rabbit would take, the children can follow on their own worksheets, thus developing effectively the eye movement needed for reading.

Color Lift-Off Is Introduced

Third grade teachers at South Olive Elementary School in West Palm Beach, Florida, have found the color lift transparency film helpful to their students. For example, Figure 5.11 demonstrates one such use.

The illustrations are clipped from a magazine that would allow color transfer onto color lift film (see Chapter 2). The pictures are

Figure 5.11. The transparency is reproduced on color lift-off film to make the illustrations more realistic. As you can see, the transparency is used in the teaching of vowel sounds.

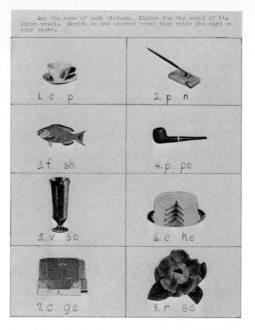

cut out and pasted onto a blank white sheet of paper, and the lettering is written in by the teacher. This original is then transferred to color lift film by use of the infrared copying machine.

As we have stressed continually throughout this book, imagination plays an important part in the use of the overhead projector in the classroom. By "imagination" is not meant complexity or ostentation but, instead, simplicity and good taste.

Figure 5.12. This is an example of how one teacher used her imagination to bring out the use of a vowel sound. Simple, but effective, is the only way to describe it.

85

Could anything be more effective in teaching vowel sounds than the transparency seen in Figure 5.12, prepared at the South Olive Elementary School? The figures' faces are colored yellow after the transparency is made on direct image positive transparency film, but the eyes representing the letter *O,* which is the theme of the lesson, are outlined in black crayon. Clear, simple and yet dramatic, this type of transparency adds considerably to interest in the lesson and to student comprehension.

Uses of Projection in Reading Summed Up

Reading teachers at St. Aloysius in Bowling Green, Ohio, also get much mileage from a bit of imagination and an overhead projector. In submitting samples, these teachers also submitted a compendium of the ways in which projection is used by them. We offer this here, since it sums up for you some of the general uses of overhead projection in the reading room (note that we said *some of the uses.* It's impossible, as you're well aware, to list all since at anytime *now* you could think of a new one):

1. In all grades, but more especially in grades 1 to 3, new words, phrases, and sentences are prepared on transparencies prior to the class period. After use with one group, they are filed away for use later with other groups. Having work prepared before class saves the teacher much daily time formerly spent in putting this work on the chalkboard.

2. The projector is used for developing eye span and for teaching the idea of the left to right sequence. A line of a story might be exposed for a short period and then removed.

3. It is also used as a speed reading device in this same way. The reading time is accurately controlled by the teacher.

4. After a story or portion is read silently from the assigned book, questions are placed on the projector as a guide for discussing what was read or as a silent reading test. The projector is particularly applicable to this use in grades 3 to 6.

5. The projector is most effectively used in reading mechanics—that is, dictionary work, spelling, and phonics. In this, individual pupils are allowed to work at the machine, while the lesson is still of much profit to class members in their seats. In the visual recognition of syllables, digraphs, compound words, and other work assigned as new or review to each grade, the value students receive from actual participation in the lesson is enhanced by overhead projection.

6. A projector is deemed invaluable to primary teachers in giving directions for worksheets completed as seatwork by the children. A transparency is made of the page assigned, for example, and then the teacher demonstrates the work on the projector. This is followed by the students in their seats doing the work. Following this teacher demonstration, the child has a better understanding of what is expected and should be able to do the work independently.

Revelation Is Employed to Check Speed-Reading

One specific example offered by St. Aloysius reading teachers to check speed-reading and comprehension is most interesting. It involves employment of the so-called revelation technique.

An original, listing several different directional sentences, is prepared on white paper and reproduced onto a sheet of transparency film (Figure 5.13). The teacher cuts strips of opaque white paper and tapes each strip in place across each of the sentences on the transparency. She hinges each strip to the side of the transparent material, so any one of the sentences can be revealed without revealing the others.

In the class, the teacher exposes only one sentence for a limited time by flipping back its opaque cover. Since the cover strips are opaque, they hide the projected image until they are removed from the trans-

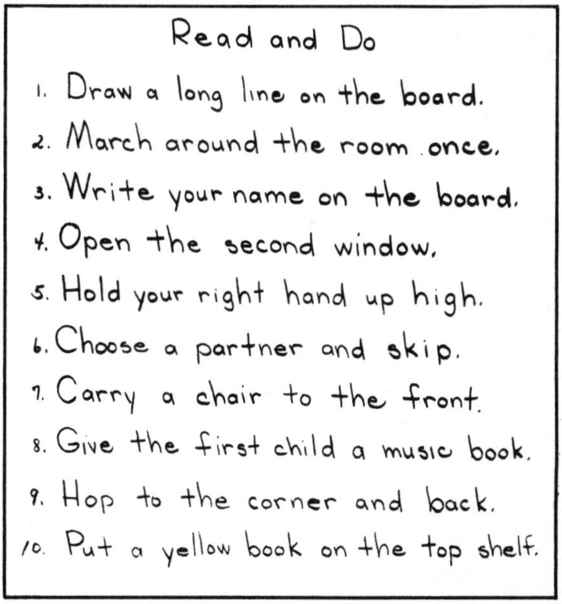

Figure 5.13. This transparency is used to check speed-reading and to give children practice in following directions. It is revealed piecemeal.

Read and Do
1. Draw a long line on the board.
2. March around the room once.
3. Write your name on the board.
4. Open the second window.
5. Hold your right hand up high.
6. Choose a partner and skip.
7. Carry a chair to the front.
8. Give the first child a music book.
9. Hop to the corner and back.
10. Put a yellow book on the top shelf.

parency. The desired sentence is projected for a limited time and then covered again. The teacher calls upon a pupil to fulfill the command.

A different way of employing revelation—actually a method that uses a modified revelation technique combined with a modified overlay technique—is used in reading classes at the California Avenue School in Uniondale, New York. The purpose of the lesson is to assist children in attacking words through initial consonants and initial consonant blends. Since this technique is also employed for special class children in the intermediate area, the teacher employing it was prompted to say, "The visual aspect of this lesson is particularly helpful to mentally retarded children."

The transparency is prepared by reproducing several small pictures and several consonant and consonant blends onto transparency film. These are cut out into small, equal size blocks.

Figure 5.14a. This is the basic transparency used in teaching consonant and consonant blends. The technique employs both revelation and overlay.

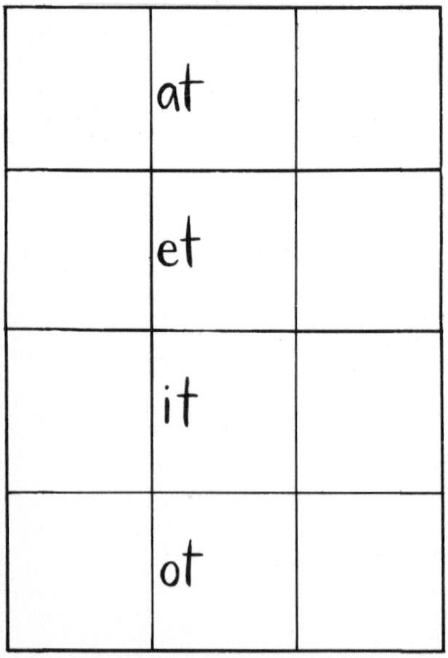

Figure 5.14b. By putting a consonant into position, a word is formed and projected.

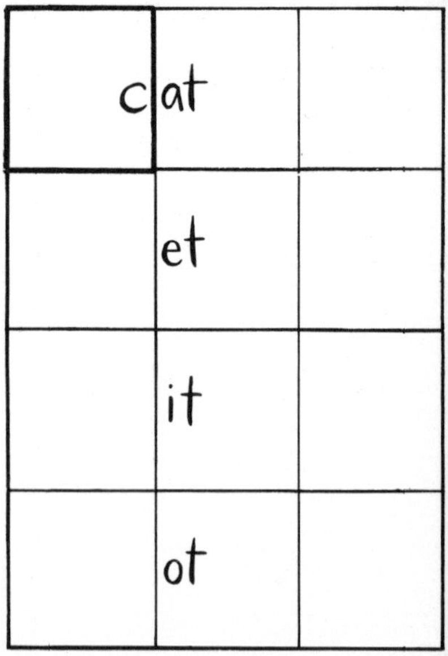

	at	
	et	
	it	
	ot	

c	at	
	et	
	it	
	ot	

On another sheet of transparency film (and in the middle of this sheet), word endings are reproduced. The consonant and consonant blends and small pictures are then matched to the larger transparency in proper relationship to the word endings.

Thus, the presentation is actually composed of three sections. On the left are the several consonant and consonant blends which, when lined up with a word ending in the middle of the transparency, make words. On the right are pictures corresponding with the several words.

In use, the transparency is placed on the projector (Figure 5.14a). The teacher speaks about one of the endings, for example, the establishment of the sound *at*. The first consonant is put into place on the transparency next to the word ending to make the word *cat*, for example (Figure 5.14b). This is discussed and the picture showing a cat is

Figure 5.14c. The picture illustrating the word is then projected, so children can associate the word with something they have seen and know.

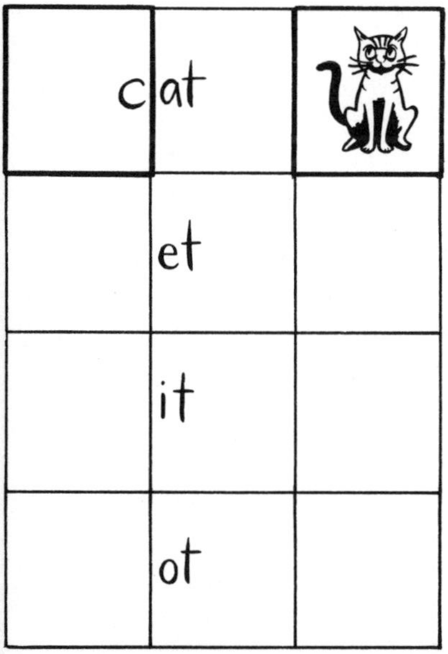

Figure 5.14d. The first consonant is removed and another consonant is put into position to show a new word and to impress the children with the fact that the new word is formed simply by changing one letter.

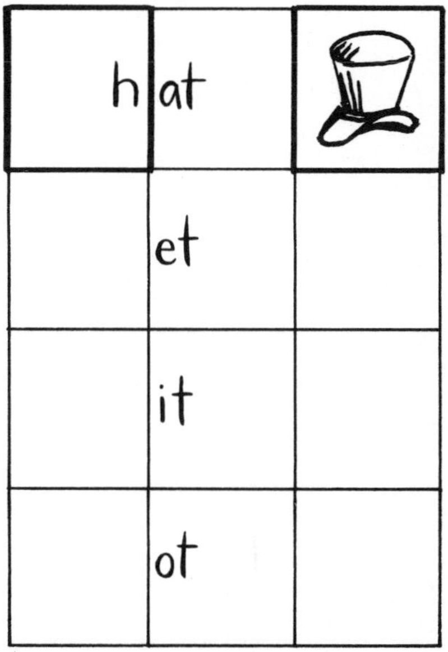

revealed (Figure 5.14c). After the discussion, the first letter and picture are removed and the next letter is put into place to show that by changing one letter a new word is formed (Figure 5.14d). This process is continued down the page.

The important role that overhead projection can play in a reading room was perhaps best described by reading teachers at School No. 8 in Buffalo, New York. Uppermost in these teachers' minds, as it should be in the minds of all teachers, is the fact that it is *the teacher* who teaches. Overhead projection is used only as a *supplement* to teaching. *It is a tool; it is not a teacher.*

But it is an important tool, as attested to by the School No. 8 teachers. Here is what they have to say concerning its employment in the reading room:

> The physical, social, emotional, and mental maturity of a child influences his readiness to read. Ability to read effectively is the keystone to education and a fruitful life. The importance of reading becomes even more obvious when one considers what happens in our culture to those who fail to learn to read well.
>
> A very important factor in a reading program is to provide children with a background of meaningful experiences. Clear, vivid, and first-hand sensory experience is the best way to develop accurate concepts. However, due to limitations of time and inaccessibility, many of our children do not have sufficient first-hand experiences which are helpful in developing reading skills.
>
> Through the use of the overhead projector and supplementary equipment, it is possible for us to bring into the classroom a variety of worthwhile experiences to enrich the background of the children. Children are eager to learn about things they have heard about but never seen. Many concepts are developed through the use of objects, graphs, and pictures.
>
> For example, to develop the concept of a music hall, a scene of the interior of a music hall can be projected on the screen and discussed. Children may then dramatize the scene by arranging their seats as in the transparency and pretend they are at the music hall. To make this more realistic, a musical record may be played while the picture is projected. In addition, while the record is playing, silhouettes of specific instruments may be shown on the screen.
>
> A similar procedure could be followed to give children vicarious experiences in or at a restaurant, bank, circus, ball game, airport, farm, railroad, weather station, etc.

Skills necessary for successful reading are developed sequentially from the time the child comes to elementary school through the grades. Comprehensive vocabulary development begins with auditory and visual discrimination in readiness classes. It is very important for children to learn the left to right eye movement. A combined auditory, visual, and muscular approach to new words in the beginning stages of learning to read may assure children success in the important task of recognizing words. Overhead projection does, of course, make the visual processes possible.

6.

Use of the Overhead Projector
in the Teaching of the Language Arts

The ability to communicate is an art which often eludes mankind. Several philosophers contend that conflicts between nation-states, both past and present, as well as conflicts within a nation-state are heightened by the inability of man to make his ideas and beliefs crystal-clear in the minds of other men.

Whether or not there is justification for this philosophy is not for us to say. However, it is a basic truth that in this era of technology and in the era of greater technology predicted for the future man must be able to express himself clearly and distinctly, with no possibility for misinterpretation.

Of what use, for example, is the most wondrous idea for an invention if the inventor is not able to communicate his plans, both verbally and in written form, to persons in a production capacity, who can take the idea and transform it into hardware?

Where do people begin to develop an understanding, appreciation, and use of language? No where else but in the classroom. To this end, a teacher might be the stimulus that enables a budding inventor, world leader, writer, doctor, or philosopher, to communicate his thoughts for the betterment of mankind.

And what about the child who will grow up to be the so-called average man? Is his ability to communicate effectively and be receptive to others who communicate less important than those who will have the responsibility for leadership? Not at all, since the fulfillment of the full life for every man depends upon his ability to talk, and write, and read.

Each teacher has at his or her disposal endless forms of material on which to base the teaching of communicating, which we now call the language arts. It could be an ordinary newspaper clipping, or a page from a periodical, or a written business letter, or a single symbolic letter from the alphabet to show correct writing form, or a sentence diagram to stress the importance and correctness of grammar, or a series of flash cards to instill correct spelling into students.

Whatever form the teaching material takes, the teacher must also determine the best way to present it—the best way to communicate with her students—so that the impact of every single lesson is implanted forever in the mind of the student. One of the more effective and modern tools for the communication of subject matter is the overhead projector. You will be able to see this for yourself as we refer to methods already in use by your colleagues who have the responsibility of teaching the language arts in schools throughout the nation.

Before citing specific examples, however, let us propose some general observations concerning areas of the language arts and projection. One area of language arts specifically suited for overhead projection, among others, is vocabulary development, which serves as the basis for communication in society.

In his work, *Programed Vocabulary: Steps Toward Improved Word Power*, Dr. James I. Brown, Professor of Rhetoric at the University of Minnesota, theorizes that vocabulary should be taught through a gradual sequence of steps. From Figure 6.1a, which is a sample page from the above mentioned work, you will notice how this gradualism takes place.

Each frame or box presents a bit of information and asks a critical question to which the student must actively respond. The student checks his written answer when he moves to the next frame, being reinforced if he is right or corrected if he is wrong. The result is a steady accumulation of a sound vocabulary in a short period of time.

The method is ideally suited to projection. Transparencies containing the sequence of steps used in building vocabulary can be projected and the revelation technique used to flash each step in order. This is done by covering the transparency with an opaque sheet and moving it gradually downward to reveal one frame at a time.

Illustrating poetry by means of projection is an excellent method for impressing into the minds of students the poem under study. For example, placing leaves on the projector stage and having their silhouettes

3. If marriage to many is polygamy, what would you call marriage to one?

monogamy

4. If *di-* is a Greek prefix meaning "twice," the word *digamy* probably means "twice _ _ _ _ _ _ _."

married

5. If *deutero-* means "second," *deuterogamy* probably means "married a _ _ _ _ _ _ time."

second

6. How many colors would you expect to see in a monochrome?

one

Figure 6.1a. This example taken from *Programed Vocabulary* by Dr. James I. Brown, which stresses gradual development of vocabulary, is suited for projection.

projected onto a screen would indeed make an indelible impression on the mind of pupils who are studying *A Leaf Falls by* e. e. cummings.

There are many other applications for projection in the language arts that one can think of. Many involve straight projection of material, many others, imaginative devices. To best summarize all, we now turn to specific uses of projection in the language arts made by teachers throughout the country.

Projection Techniques

Language arts teachers at St. James High School in Grand Forks, North Dakota, list eleven ways in which overhead projection is used in their classrooms. By no means all-inclusive, this list does, however, sum up for us certain subject material that can be employed because of projection:

1. We project different styles of letters and forms for papers. This, of course, is not possible to do without overhead projection unless we duplicated each style or form and passed it out to each student, which is too time consuming.

2. We project correct arrangement of bibliographies and footnotes prior to assigning the writing of term papers.

3. We correct individual themes under the eyes of students.

4. We improve student penmanship by showing samples of acceptable and good styles of handwriting as opposed to poor and unacceptable styles found in students' papers.

5. We project whole poems for analysis by students.

6. We project whole paragraphs for analysis.

7. We project different writing styles of various authors for comparison and analysis.

8. We are able to analyze newspaper and magazine articles because of projection.

9. We are able to demonstrate different types of outline forms by means of projection.

10. We project pictures related to units of study.

11. We project pages from magazines with which we want students to become acquainted.

Use of Projection in Theme Correction

According to St. James language arts teachers, "probably the most important asset of the overhead projector to us is its assistance in theme

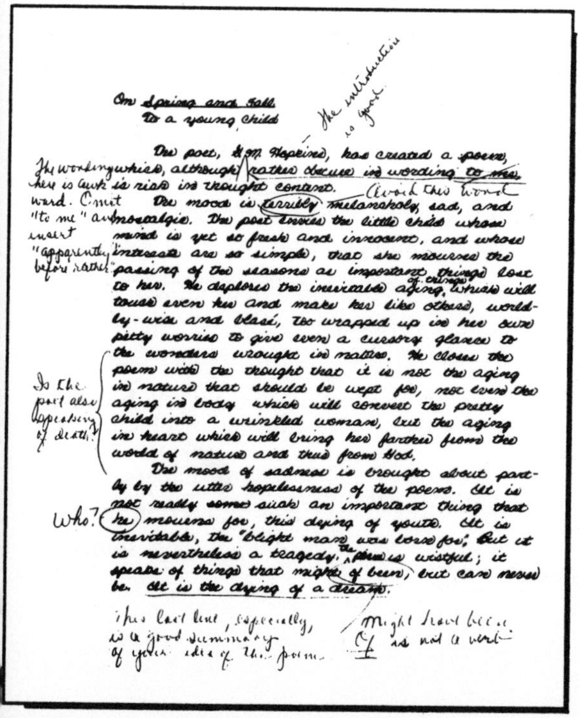

On Spring and Fall
To a young Child

The poet, G. M. Hopkins, has created a poem, which, although rather obscure in wording to me, is rich in thought content.

The mood is terribly melancholy, sad, and nostalgic. The poet knows the little child whose mind is yet so fresh and innocent, and whose interests are so simple, that she mourns the passing of the seasons as important things lost to her. He deplores the inevitable aging of things, which will touch even her and make her like others, worldly-wise and blasé, too wrapped up in her own petty worries to give even a cursory glance to the wonders wrought in nature. He closes the poem with the thought that it is not the aging in nature that should be wept for, not even the aging in body which will convert the pretty child into a wrinkled woman, but the aging in heart which will bring her farther from the world of nature and thus from God.

The mood of sadness is brought about partly by the utter hopelessness of the poem. It is not really some such an important thing that he mourns for, this dying of youth. It is inevitable, the "blight man was born for." But it is nevertheless a tragedy. The poem is wistful; it speaks of things that might of been, but can never be. It is the dying of a dream.

Figure 6.1b. Students learn by seeing. When they view mistakes they've made in writing a theme, chances are good that they will not make the same mistake again.

correction." The teacher projects a student theme already corrected and points out errors to show how the paper can be improved; this way the class as a whole benefits from the critique. Or, she corrects a composition paper right on the projector, in full view of the students, so the entire class can see the actual procedure.

To do these things, the teacher simply takes a student's paper, puts it into contact with a sheet of direct positive image transparency film, and runs both through an infrared machine. In just four seconds, she has a reproduction of the paper which she places on the projector stage. She uses a grease pencil to make any notations she wants to stress.

Figure 6.1b is an example of an actual student paper submitted in a 12th grade English class that was used as the basis of a critique by means of the overhead projector.

The value of using overhead projection to correct and critique student themes is attested to by teachers at Elizabeth Seton High School in Pittsburgh, Pennsylvania.

"My classes agree unanimously," a teacher says, "that correcting and evaluating student themes before their eyes have helped them more than any other device to understand their weaknesses and overcome them."

Projection Used in Poetry Study

Another use of projection at Elizabeth Seton High is found in the teaching of poetry. The poem to be studied is reproduced on transparency film and projected. This transparency is covered with a sheet of unexposed, clear transparency film or acetate on which the teacher is able to underscore with grease pencil such things as scansion, rhyme scheme, and metrical innovation. On another clear overlay, and again with grease pencil, she underscores significant words, images, assonance, and consonance.

"The use of the overlays," she states, "permits the reviewing of the poem without the marks used for explication. Students respond better to this method of explication than to that of any other presentation I know. Spirit master copies to be marked or textbook copies of poems are much less satisfactory since there is no way for the attention of the whole class to be on the one copy of the poem."

Differences in writing style are also effectively presented by means of overhead projection. Figure 6.2 shows a transparency used at Elizabeth Seton High to stress that shorter sentences could be vigorous and effective.

Each writer has his own little peculiarities of style. Avoid "primer style" choppy sentences, but sometimes shorter sentences are vigorous and effective.

J E S U S W E P T.

R O M E B U R N E D.

T H E F I GH T W A S O N.

T W O M E N I H O N O R-- A N D N O M O R E.

SARAH BATTLE WAS A GENTLEWOMAN BORN.

THE CHILDREN OF ALICE CALL BARTRUM FATHER.

THERE IS A LAND OF THE LIVING AND A LAND OF THE DEAD. AND THE BRIDGE IS LOVE.

Figure 6.2. A transparency to emphasize differences in writing style imparts the message to the student clearly, effectively, and forcefully.

Projection Permits Introduction of Comics

Who said that comic strips have no place in the language arts class? Teachers at Winfield Street Elementary School in Corning, New York, believe otherwise, and prove it.

The illustrations seen in Figures 6.3 and 6.4 demonstrate comic strip use. To prepare the transparency, the teacher first takes a comic strip (Figure 6.3) and blocks out the narrative contained in the balloons with opaque white paper (Figure 6.4). She then reproduces it in transparency form and projects it without narrative.

According to the teacher, a comic strip is an effective aid in teaching narrative-type exposition. By means of the projection, student ability in learning to write direct quotations, in paragraphing when the speaker changes, and in combining description with direct quotations is enhanced.

The teacher projects the comic without the balloons and motivates the children by allowing them to guess at the story and conversation. As the lesson progresses, the teacher and class write a story in paragraph form based on the projection. The "mechanics" involved in writing are stressed as the teacher transcribes the story onto the chalkboard.

Winfield Street Elementary teachers explain that there is an important byproduct to this method. "Many comic strips, with balloons removed, are quite nondescript and open-ended," they state.

"A classroom of pupils might 'tell' and 'add to' the story, projecting their own feelings, fears, inhibitions, etc. The skillful teacher, guidance counselor, or psychologist could direct the discussion by adding one or a few balloons. This opens up all sorts of possibilities for constructive group discussion."

Figure 6.3.

Figure 6.4.

Use of Projection to Teach Writing

"Utilization of the overhead projector is highly effective in the teaching of writing in ninth grade English classes at Westlake Junior High," a teacher from that school, located in Erie, Pennsylvania, explains. "Not only can errors in work be shown to the class, but also examples of acceptable writing. The former give students an opportunity to view errors *and* corrections at the same time, thus informing them of possible solutions to problems immediately. Good writing, thus displayed, might serve to motivate students to improve the quality of their own work in order that it be more acceptable."

To illustrate this proposition, the following lesson in writing was sub-

mitted. Chief aim of the lesson is development of topic sentences and variety of sentence beginnings.

Students are asked to consider a projected paragraph (Figure 6.5a). Word order in each sentence is pointed out, with each *sentence beginning* being a subject/predicate type.

Students are asked to point out errors, as follows:

Sentence 1—misplaced modifier (still)
Sentence 3—capitalization (classical)
Sentence 4—omission of commas (adjective clause)
Sentence 4—agreement of subject and predicate
Sentence 7—spelling (variety)
Sentence 7—misuse of period

Figure 6.5a. This transparency is the initial one used in a lesson concerned with writing. It also contains various errors which the class is asked to find.

WAYS TO BEGIN ENGLISH SENTENCES

1.	Subject alone	John drove his car.
2.	Article ≠ subject	The children ran away.
3.	Adjective ≠ subject	Large trees require much water.
4.	Adverb before subject	Quickly the windows were closed.
5.	Prepositional phrase first	
	as an adjective	From my class, only two boys were chosen to attend the meeting.
	as an adverb	From the edge of the woods we could see the calm and peaceful lake.
6.	Participial phrase first	
	Present participle	Taking a short-cut, the boy soon reached the fair-grounds.
	Past participle	His work completed, the janitor locked the doors and left.
	Perfect participle	Having examined all the maps, I chose a route which avoided large cities.
7.	Infinitive as subject	To win was his first consideration.
8.	Gerund as subject	Swimming is great fun.
9.	Postponed subjects	There are six rules in that club.
10.	Adverbial clause	When the train came in, I searched for my brother.
11.	Noun clause first	How he could avoid doing his chores puzzled the lazy boy.
12.	Verb first (To be used only for great emphasis!)	Arrived at last the long awaited day!
13.	Object first	A fresh start, the student decided he must have.
14.	Conjunction first	But the last was best of all!
15.	Expletive first	Well, that is finally done. Alas, we have no food for dinner

Figure 6.5c. A transparency that sums up the points made during the lesson is then flashed and studied.

Paragraph I

(1) The Renaissance still is something of a mystery to historians. (2) We can point to certain superficial qualities of the period. (3) There was a revival of interest in the Classical world during the Renaissance. (4) The literature of Greece and Rome which had been neglected for so many years were translated and read throughout Europe. (5) We associate the rebellion against ecclesiastical authority an example of Renaissance thinking. (6) This rebellion made one feel freer to think for himself. (7) The Renaissance was a period in which a variety of points of view were possible. (8) But they had unity of thought. (9) This period is associated with the rise of Modern Science. (10) A complete shift in the attitude toward the investigation of the world around us.

Figure 6.5b. Students are given the opportunity to study various ways to begin sentences.

Paragraph II

Though the Renaissance is still something of a mystery to historians, we can, nevertheless, point to certain superficial qualities by which it is possible to characterize the period. First of all, during the Renaissance there was a revival of interest in the classical world. After many years of neglect, the literature of Greece and Rome was now translated and read throughout Europe. Rebelling against ecclesiastical authority is a second development that we associate with this period. To think for himself became man's foremost ambition as a result of this rebellion. Consequently, the Renaissance was a period in which a variety of points of view were possible. Having unity of thought, however, is a characteristic of the Middle Ages. Finally, this period is associated with the rise of modern science, a complete shift in the attitude toward the investigation of the world around us.

Sentence 8—incomplete (awkward) construction
Sentence 9—capitalization (modern science)
Sentence 10—non-sentence

Students are then asked to improve the topic sentence, as well as all other sentences, in light of improving sentence beginnings. As an aid, a transparency listing ways of beginning English sentences is projected and discussed (Figure 6.5b).

Finally, an improved work (Figure 6.5c) is projected. Variety in sentence beginnings, development of topic sentence, and techniques in paragraphing are stressed. Furthermore, the improved transition demonstrated by means of the transparency is used as a base of comparison and contrast by the class.

The teacher using this effective method states the following:

"These procedures are most effective in team teaching, which is, actually, simply a group procedure intended to ensure the most profitable use both of pupil and teacher time. Students with writing difficulties are grouped according to major problems. Transparencies similar to the ones seen are made to solve these difficulties. The more able students are given materials which would be of a more advanced nature, and as such would challenge them to the fullest. Grouping on this basis avoids the deadly effects of repetition and boredom for students."

Using Projection in Oral Story-Telling

Oral story-telling is without peer in getting young elementary school children in the habit of communicating with their classmates. Such a technique is employed by language arts teachers at Battell Elementary School in Mishawaka, Indiana.

The teacher examines magazines, workbooks and other material for pictures and illustrations that could be related one to the other in story form. She clips these out and reproduces each on a transparency for projection. *The Story of Petey*, prepared for the fifth grade, is an excellent example.

The story's length and development suggest that it can be used for many separate lessons in oral story-telling. How soon new pictures are revealed to change and develop the plot depends on the class and the success with which they handle this type of exercise. Needless to say, the children look forward with expectation to seeing a new picture.

The story could develop in the following manner:

Project Transparency #1 (Figure 6.6a)—Petey is a Dennis the menace type, lovable but always in the midst of excitement. His lazy dog, Zip, always trails along, adding to the general confusion.

Project Transparency #2 (Figure 6.6b)—Petey has a pet hamster.

Project Transparency #3 (Figure 6.6c)—One day when the hamster got loose, Petey broke his mother's prized antique pitcher as he dashed through the house in pursuit of the animal. After moments of agony, he succeeded in repairing the pitcher by gluing and tying it together. Naturally, his mother was very upset.

As you can see, no other teaching tool provides the versatility, flexibility, and satisfactory results needed to introduce oral story-telling into the classroom as does the overhead projector.

A simple diagram drawn on a piece of transparency film and projected for two minutes is sometimes more effective in getting a point

Figure 6.6a. Cartoon-type characters are useful in teaching elementary school students the fundamentals of oral communication.

Figure 6.6b. Each character is designed to follow the previous one and have some meaning when viewed in relation to the others so children can tie them together in story form.

THIS IS PETEY.

YOU CAN ALWAYS COUNT ON HIM
TO STIR UP A LITTLE EXCITEMENT.

**mom,
what'll i do now?**

THIS IS PETEY'S DOG, ZIP.

ZIP IS LAZY, AND AT TIMES NOT VERY BRIGHT.

across than a 40-minute discussion. Take Figure 6.7 as an example. It is a transparency which was prepared at Garfield High School in Akron, Ohio.

As you can see, the diagram illustrates the differences between Shakespearean, Greek, and modern play structure and is used as an introduction to the drama.

Using Projection to Teach Grammar

Teaching the fundamentals of diagramming sentences and thus the fundamentals of grammar to elementary school children is particularly suitable to overhead projection techniques because of the ability to use overlays. At Sunset Elementary School in Selah, Washington, for example, the technique seen in Figures 6.8a, 6.8b, and 6.8c is used.

A list of sentences designed to teach subject/predicate relation is

Figure 6.6c. These originals can be reproduced on any type of transparent film and colored, if desired.

Figure 6.7. Not even a 40-minute class discussion could do more in comparing types of drama for students as does this simple projection.

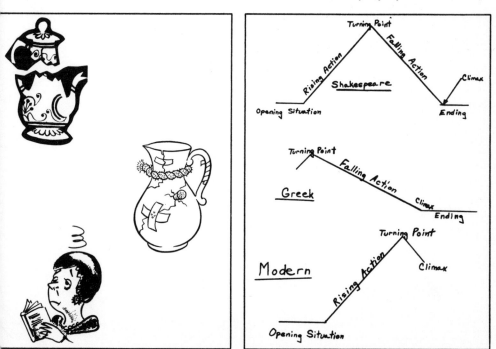

Figure 6.8a. This transparency, listing sentences that are simple subject/predicate in form, is the basic transparency in an overlay system to teach the rudiments of grammar.

Diagraming sentences.

Subjects and Predicates

A peasant girl lived in France.

Joan loved her country.

The King led the army.

Her cousin listened to her story.

Sir Robert laughed at her.

The people gave money for clothing.

Two young noblemen went along.

Her guides followed side roads.

King Charles thought she was a witch.

---

sheet No. 2

Subjects

A peasant girl |

Joan |

The King |

Her cousin |

Sir Robert |

The people |

Two young noblemen |

Her guides |

King Charles |

Figure 6.8b. The first overlay presents the subjects.

Figure 6.8c. The second overlay presents the predicate portion.

---

sheet N

Predicates

lived in France

loved her country

led the army

listened to her story

laughed at her

gave money for clothing

went along

followed side roads

thought she was a witch

104

presented by means of the projector (Figure 6.8a). Overlay No. 1 is the subject sheet and is laid over the basic transparency (Figure 6.8b). Overlay No. 2 is the predicate sheet and is laid over the basic transparency and overlay No. 1. Naturally, the same technique can be employed as diagramming becomes more complex. But remember the principle of simplicity. It might be best to show the diagramming of only one sentence on a transparency, using different colored pencils to outline individual grammatical forms.

Dictionary Skills Taught by Projection

At Howard W. Bishop Junior High School in Gainsville, Florida, an eight-day unit designed to develop in students a desire to use the dictionary skillfully and efficiently was prepared. By means of the unit, the value of a dictionary as a rich source of varied information was brought to the student's attention. Impact was added by means of colorful projections.

The following materials were used in development of the unit:

1. An 11-minute Coronet film entitled, *We Discover the Dictionary*.
2. A dictionary for each student.
3. A classroom unabridged dictionary.
4. An overhead projector and colored grease pencils.
5. A group of seven transparencies.

At the outset of the lesson, the film and individual student examination of the dictionary were employed to introduce the study. The lesson then evolved in the following manner:

• *Kinds of dictionaries.* Comparison of the abridged and unabridged dictionary was illustrated by the use of a mimeographed sheet. On one half of the sheet was a word and meaning copied from an abridged dictionary while on the other half was a similar segment from an unabridged dictionary. The comparison between the two was easily seen by the students.

• *Locating a word.* Transparency No. 1 was used with colored grease pencils to explain alphabetizing to the second, third and fourth letters (Figure 6.9a). After this segment of the lesson, transparency No. 2 was used to flash words, and each student participated in a speed drill in finding the words in the dictionary (Figure 6.9b). The purpose of

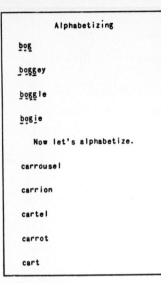

Alphabetizing
bog
boggey
boggle
bogie
Now let's alphabetize.
carrousel
carrion
cartel
carrot
cart

look up these words
recalcitrant
topgallant
toril
zirconium
reclamation
flounce
misfeasance

Syllables	
corps	one syllable
cor_ral	two syllable
cos_met_ic	three syllab
con_cen_tra_tion	four syllab
cos_mo_pol_i_tan	five syllab
Divide into syllables	
cosignatory	
loosen	
musketeer	
reasonable	

Figure 6.9a. This transparency shows alphabetizing of words, and also gives students an exercise to perform under teacher supervision.

Figure 6.9b. This transparency forms the basis of a speed drill for the students in looking up words in the dictionary. Words on the transparency should be revealed one at a time. They can be covered with a sheet of plain white paper until time for revelation.

Figure 6.9c. This transparency is used as a basis for a discussion of syllabication.

this segment of the lesson was to encourage students to keep a mental picture of the word as they searched for it.

● *Information provided in the dictionary.*

1. *Syllabication.* Transparency No. 3 was shown to reveal several examples of words divided into syllables (Figure 6.9c). Words were then dictated to the class for student practice. A volunteer was called upon to put the correct syllable division on the transparency and each student was encouraged to correct his own work from the visible example.

2. *Pronunciation.* Transparency No. 4 was shown to demonstrate how helpful and necessary a dictionary is for correct pronunciation (Figure 6.9d). Students participated by finding the correct pronunciation of the words in their dictionaries. Transparency No. 5 provided a color key to teach the markings one finds in a dictionary and their meanings (Figure 6.9e).

corps	door	corpse
wan	don	man
wary	hairy	tarry
fiend	reined	leaned
indict	verdict	polite

Figure 6.9d. This transparency is used as a basis for a discussion of pronunciation.

— long vowel	fōlder
⌣ short vowel	lĕtter
ə schwa	⌣ə pencil
╱ accents	eléctricity

mark these words:

denomination

manufacture

comparison

dictionary

Figure 6.9e. Naturally, meanings of dictionary symbols are important. The transparency is used to teach these.

SAMPLE SECTION

as-sign′ment (ă-sīn′mĕnt),n. 1. Legal transfer of property by one person to another; as, he made an assignment for the benefitof his creditors. 2. Property assigned by one person to another.

as sim′i-late (ă-sim′ĭ lāt), v.t. & i. (L. assimilatus, past part. of assimilare, fr. ad- + similare to make like, fr. similis like 1. To make or become similar or alike. 2. To take up and absorb (food) assimilable , adj.

as-sist′ (ă-sĭst′), v. i. & t. (fr. F., fr. L. assistere, fr. ad- + sistere to cause to stand , fr. stare to stand.) To lend or give aid; to help; aid.--- Syn. See HELP n. An assisting; aid.

as-sist′ant (-tănt), adj. That assists; specif. acting as a subordinate. --n. 1. A helper 2. A means of help; an aid.

Figure 6.9f. This transparency provides a basis for a discussion on roots, derivatives, and word origins.

troublemakers

agreeable	ninety
bargain	poetry
beginning	responsible
benefit	sensible
candidate	sincerely
carrying	stopped
comfortable	therefore
courage	together
handkerchief	truly
individual	writing

Figure 6.9g. Word demons are projected, and the teacher provides rules for remembering the spelling of such words.

3. *Meanings.* At this point, different meanings for the same word are emphasized. To point this out clearly, the teacher refers to "Semantics as a Common Language" from *Teaching Secondary English* by John J. DeBaer, Walter Kaulfers and Helen Miller. She provides various examples as, for instance, "The word *run* has over 800 meanings."

4. *Roots, Derivatives and Origins.* Transparency No. 6 is projected. It is a copy of a dictionary page and is used to illustrate the ways in which roots, derivatives and origins are designated (Figure 6.9f).

5. *Spelling.* Transparency No. 7 is projected to present a list of word demons. The teacher uses a grease pencil to mark the transparency while it is on the projector stage, being projected, to show students aids for remembering such words (Figure 6.9g).

• *Review.* The class is asked to develop a dictionary page on a transparency using all items presented in the unit. Individual transparencies are projected and a critique is held.

• *Evaluation.* Transparency No. 6 or one similar to it is used again as a testing device. Students are shown the transparency and are asked to label it and explain the particular items covered during the lesson.

Using the Projector to Analyze Writing

"Aside from the obvious, frequent, and invaluable use of the overhead projector in discussing the students' own compositions, there lies the splendid opportunity of analyzing any piece of writing from an innumerable sequence of viewpoints," teachers at Chaminade High School in Dayton, Ohio, contend.

The way this is done is to select at random writings from magazines, periodicals, journals or what have you, make transparencies of them and, using colored grease pencils, mark off on the transparency and comment about such characteristics of good writing as use of a variety of sentence types, use of a variety of sentence lengths, avoidance of unnecessary shifts in subject and verb, utilization of parallel structure, and possession of unity and emphasis.

Figure 6.10 is an excellent illustration of how this method is utilized. Objective of the lesson was to see how a composition reflects a variety of sentence types. On the transparency, a complex sentence is outlined in red, a compound sentence is outlined in green, a compound-complex

COMPLEX	SUDDENLY YOU see Oxford, a gray blur in the valley, as you drive over the hill from Newbury and the south. A haze of smoke, age, and legend veils her, a lo-
COMPOUND	comotive snorts in her railway sidings, and all around her lie the moist green hills of the Midlands, like open lettuce leaves. Visionary and beckoning
COMPLEX	stand her spires and domes, as Judge the Obscure glimpsed them long ago, for Oxford possesses always the quality of an idea.

SIMPLE — She is more than a city, more than a railroad station, more than a road junction, more even than a university. She epitomizes a remarkable kingdom, here in the belly of England; she is a shrine to the truth, where many a fine soul has worshiped; she is a paradigm of the human conflict between the right and the wrong, the spiritual and the material, the ugly and the beautiful; and most of all she is an aspiration, a sad reminder of what the world might be—the turn of a phrase and the joy of a discovery and the smile of a pretty girl in a punt.

COMPOUND-COMPLEX

COMPOUND — Her comprehension transcends classes and races and grasps the whole range of human experience, from the sublime to the rock bottom. She has been fouled by

SIMPLE — time and degradation. She has been fortified by centuries of controversy, rivalry,

SIMPLE — and rancor. She stands beyond everyday logic, crooked, deep, and contradictory.

SIMPLE

COMPLEX — She is not a large place—from your bump in the road you may see the whole of her, and inspect her suburbs in a sweep from Headington to Hinksey. But as an

COMPOUND-COMPLEX — Englishman in America once observed, when asked which Oxford he came from, this is not Oxford, Mississippi, nor Oxford, Nova Scotia, nor Oxford, New Zealand, nor even simply Oxford, England: this is Oxford, All the Bloody World.

—from: "Is Oxford Out of this World?" by James Morris   in Horizon, January, 1963

paradigm: a model or pattern
punt: a flat bottomed boat
degradation: process of degrading

Number of Kinds of sentences

COMPLEX ————— 3
COMPOUND ————— 2
SIMPLE ————— 4
COMPOUND-COMPLEX - 2

Figure 6.10. A simple reproduction onto transparency film of a piece of literature and a few colored pencils are all that's needed to form a basis for a discussion concerning good writing. In this case, the lesson subject was the different kinds of sentences one can find in a single piece of writing.

sentence is outlined in violet, and a simple sentence remains clear in color.

At a glance, then, the class is able to see that a composition is composed of a variety of sentence types—in this case, three complex sentences, two compound sentences, four simple sentences, and two compound-complex sentences.

In teaching the writing of a business letter, overlays can be used to good advantage, as they are at Healy Elementary School in Detroit, Michigan. The use of overlays enables you to present the business letter forms one part at a time, which helps the student to clearly understand and better retain the necessary format.

Four overlays are made: inside address, greeting, body, and closing. The *heading* forms the *basic* transparency, and the others are hinged to it in proper registration, so each can be presented one at a time. Furthermore, when all overlays are in place, the student can see the entire letter form in proper perspective.

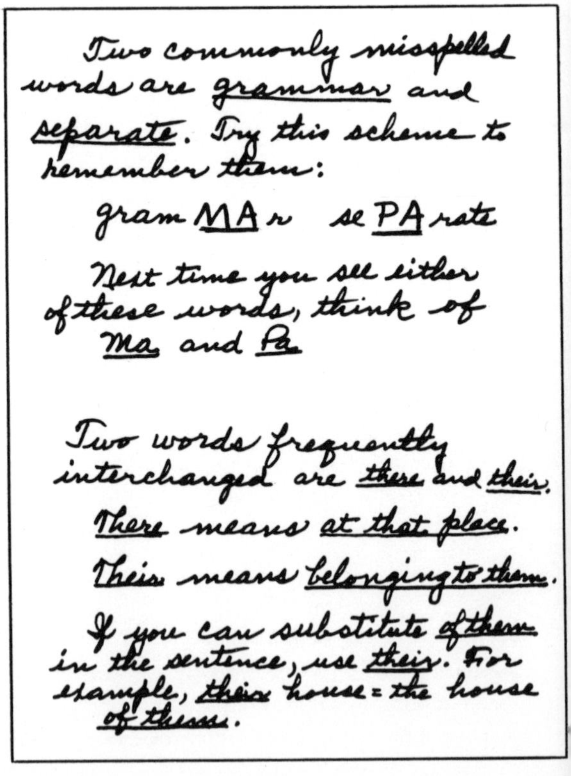

Figure 6.11. Few devices for emphasizing important points in language usage are as effective as a transparency on an overhead projector.

The teacher can leave out punctuation marks if she wishes, and mark them in on the overlays with grease pencil during projection. She can also prepare the overlays in different colors, so each part stands out when the letter is assembled.

Simplicity Is the Key

Teachers should never lose sight of the fact that they don't always have to base an entire lesson on the overhead projector. The projector employed just once during a lesson to drive home a point is equally effective.

Take, for example, the transparency seen in Figure 6.11, which was prepared at Palm Beach Public School in Palm Beach, Florida. As you can see, the one transparency deals with two areas often mis-used by students. Flashing this on a screen for a few minutes so the students can see it implants the points firmly in their minds.

7.

Use of the Overhead Projector
in the Teaching of the
Social Sciences

The broad program of study known as social sciences takes various forms according to grade level. In the lower grades, social studies encompass the teaching of history and *social* geography. (We are not concerned here with physical geography, which is a pure science.)

In junior and senior high schools, the study of history continues, but the study of geography eventually terminates and new subjects, also social scientific in nature, are introduced. Primary among these are the so-called political sciences, which in most pre-university schools are called problems of American democracy, or civics, or current events, or even politics.

When a student leaves high school and enters college, he again comes face to face with subjects that are definitive in topical matter, but which are related to and carried under the broad heading of social science. History in all its forms (western civilization, early American, early European, modern European, and so forth) and political subjects, especially political science, are, of course, ever present. But now the student encounters a new group which is social in nature. In this group are philosophy, sociology, psychology, criminology, and the like.

Thus, from the elementary school through college, social science subject is compounded upon social science subject. And we find teachers searching for new methods to bring to their students the great mountain of material which is built up from the small hill begun in the first grade.

Of course, no method yet devised has replaced the teacher's personality and his or her way of delivering the material sought by the student. However, an aid to this delivery is never out of place; in fact, it is desired and sought.

Such an aid, and perhaps the best yet conceived, is the overhead projector.

In your mind, no doubt, you have already formulated ways of using overhead projection in your history or geography class or in other classes devoted to subjects of a social scientific nature. Several of the methods we outline below might appear less sophisticated than the ones you have developed. Others will seem more complex.

For example, what better "history book" is there available for student and teacher than the daily newspaper? It is an ever-ready and constant source of up-to-date information that is not found in any current textbook.

The National Council for the Social Sciences has undertaken a program in how to use the daily newspaper. The intent is to develop in each student the habit of reading the newspaper everyday to be adequately informed about community, state, national, and world events. Another objective is to encourage the student to read carefully and probe the accounts of current events in order to discuss contemporary issues intelligently and act with good judgment.

There is no doubt that overhead projection can assist in development of these good habits. Just a news story—say of election returns, campaign issues, debates concerning conservation or rezoning ordinances, a United Nations issue, or a change in Soviet government or policy—projected onto a screen and discussed critically for the purposes of evaluating the consequences can imbue students with respect for the newspaper and what can be derived from it. As trite as it may sound, the old adage that an informed and discerning people remain a free people is as true today as it ever was.

Our intention in this chapter, as in all the chapters in this book, is to bring forth the one idea that projection, no matter how simple, is one of the greatest aids you can use in teaching. You should always judge its value to the subject material, whether it is for something as simple as projecting an outline map of the United States or a portrait of Toynbee. Projection makes the social sciences come alive in the student's mind. We will now proceed to show how.

Simple Tranparency Aids Historical Learning

"How did the United States grow?" This was the subject of an area of historical study presented to students at the Maple Ridge Elementary School in Somerset, Pennsylvania. Instead of trying to make the students form mental pictures which, at best, is difficult, the teacher employed overhead projection in a simple, but effective and picturesque manner.

She started with a basic outline map of the United States, which was reproduced onto a clear sheet of direct reading image positive film. The east and west boundaries, represented by the Atlantic and Pacific Oceans, were colored in with blue felt marker.

The projection was placed on the projector stage and shown. As each growth group was discussed, the teacher simply used a different-colored marker to color that group, and the students saw in front of them the development of their country. This was done as follows:

1. The original area of the United States to the Mississippi River—colored in light green.

2. The Louisiana Purchase—colored in dark green.

3. The bit of territory ceded by Great Britain in 1818 when the 49th parallel was established as the boundary between Canada and the United States—colored in red.

4. The Florida Purchase—colored in orange.

5. The Texas Annexation—colored in yellow.

6. The Mexican cession—colored in purple.

7. The Gadsen Purchase—colored in blue.

8. The Oregon country—colored in orange.

9. The Alaskan and Hawaiian acquisitions—colored in brown.

Although exceptionally simple to apply, this presentation is still forceful and offers the student every advantage for retention when coupled with the lecture.

More Sophisticated Methods Can Be Used

The types of transparencies used in history classes at Sedgwick Junior High School in West Hartford, Connecticut, run the gamut from simple to complex.

(Understand that the words "simple" and "complex" as used here have no connection with the proposal made in Chapter 2 of this book that transparencies should be kept simple in nature. The words "simple" and "complex" as used here connote that the transparency is either easy to prepare, requiring little time, or that it is more difficult to prepare, requiring much time in preparation. Both types show imagination in their utility and in their introduction into the lesson to support that lesson. Both types are readily palatable to a viewer, since neither offers too much for retention at any one time; this is the meaning of the word "simple" as used in Chapter 2.)

To illustrate and forcefully impart the point that the Continental Army received help from the French during the Revolutionary War, a teacher simply reproduced a page from a textbook onto direct reading image positive film (Figure 7.1). This diagram and a few lines of text enabled the student to impress on his mind this historical fact. At the same time the information as to how supplies were sent was *seen* and *retained* by the student.

Figure 7.1. This reproduction from a textbook, introduced at the right moment during a class, cannot help but make an impression on the students that the Continental Army received foreign help during the Revolution.

Under the ficticious name of Hortalez and Co., Caron de Beaumarchais helped Deane send over ninety per cent of the supplies used by the Continental Army up until Burgoyne's surrender at Saratoga.

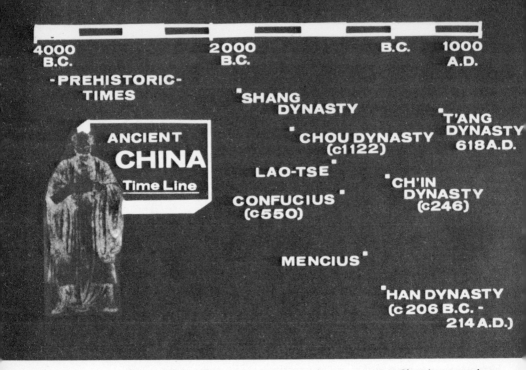

Figure 7.2. This transparency made on negative film shows students at a glance the ancient dynasties of China and when they ruled.

Of a more complicated nature is the transparency illustrated in Figure 7.2 showing the time line of ancient China for students studying ancient history. The teacher again used a page from a textbook. This time, however, he reproduced it onto direct reading image negative transparency material. As explained in Chapter 2, this material reverses the original image—that is, black on the original reproduces as clear and white on the original reproduces as black on the transparency.

At a glance, the students are able to see and take notes of how the dynasties of ancient China fitted into the development of the civilization. Certainly the medium of overhead projection saved time in eliminating the need for the teacher having to either relate this information verbally or transcribe it onto the chalkboard. Add to this the fact that projection is more effective from a teaching standpoint than either verbal orientation or chalkboard writing, and you can understand the great stress now being placed on projection techniques by school officials.

A transparency of extreme complexity, but one which is invaluable in relating facts relative to the history of transportation, is seen in Figure 7.3. The textual material was again reproduced onto direct reading image negative film. But to offset the possibility of offering

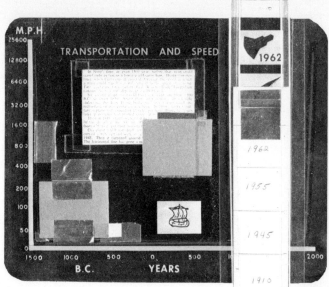

Figure 7.3. Quite complex in makeup, this transparency is nonetheless one of the most effective in relating the history of transportation. Note the revelation devices employed—specifically, cardboard flaps and plastic runners stapled to the transparent material.

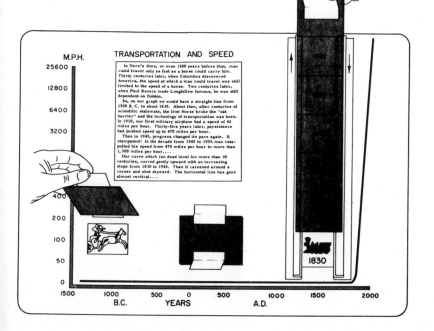

TRANSPORTATION AND SPEED

In Nero's time, or even 1500 years before that, man could travel only as fast as a horse could carry him. Thirty centuries later, when Columbus discovered America, the speed at which a man could travel was still limited to the speed of a horse. Two centuries later, when Paul Revere made Longfellow famous, he was still dependent on Dobbin.

So, on our graph we would have a straight line from 1500 B.C. to about 1830. About then, after centuries of scientific stalemate, the Iron Horse broke the "oat barrier" and the technology of transportation was born. In 1910, our first military airplane had a speed of 42 miles per hour. Thirty-five years later, persistence had pushed speed up to 470 miles per hour.

Then in 1945, progress changed its pace again. It stampeded! In the decade from 1945 to 1955 man catapulted his speed from 470 miles per hour to more than 1,500 miles per hour....

Our curve which ran dead level for more than 30 centuries, curved gently upward with an increasing slope from 1830 to 1945. Then it careened around a corner and shot skyward. The horizontal line has gone almost vertical....

too much material to the student at one time and to introduce the data at the precise moment in the lecture where they would be most effective, the teacher applied several revelation techniques.

The two illustrations in the lower left are covered with cardboard flaps. The line of illustrations to the right is covered with a strip of cardboard placed inside two plastic runners. When the appropriate moment comes, the teacher flips back the cardboard flaps or pulls up the runner to reveal the mode of transportation. The cardboard runner is "dated" for the teacher's reference.

The teacher also attached text relating to the transparency directly to the transparency for reference. Since the text is printed on opaque paper, it is not projected.

Although not visible to you, colored transparency tape was used to highlight and make more attractive areas of pictorial and textual interest.

Mapping a War by Projection

No area of history enthralls students, especially those of the male gender, as much as war. And no war holds as much interest for American students as the Civil War. Overhead projection raises that interest to still greater heights, as proven in classes of American history at Limerick School in Limerick, Maine.

Figure 7.4a. The chronological data shown here formed the basis of a study of the southern campaign during the Civil War.

Figure 7.4b. This map used in conjunction with the chronological transparency seen in Figure 7.4a made "strategists" of the students and whetted their appetite to learn.

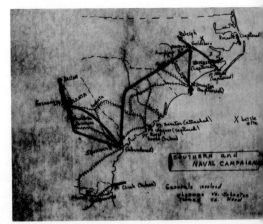

Figures 7.4a and 7.4b show just one example in relating the happenings of the Southern and naval campaigns of 1864 and 1865. Figure 7.4a is a chronological textual outline of the high points of these battles, and from it the students take notes. Figure 7.4b, a map illustrating the lines of battle, is projected alternately with the outline text to show the evolution of the campaigns. Interest is held at a high pitch as the teacher asks, "John, if you were General Sherman (or Hood, or Thomas, or Johnston), what would you have done? Come to the projector, use this grease pencil and show us."

Uses of Projection Listed

Teachers at Saint Mary's Central High School in Bismarck, North Dakota, were asked to compile a list of ten ways in which they would use overhead projection in their classrooms. The following was offered by a teacher of ancient history:

It is difficult selecting just ten items which would best illustrate for ancient history the use of an overhead projector, which I certainly believe is a definite asset to the social science department. The following ten are among many that I could think of in using this efficient machine:

1. Teaching map skills, especially supplementary maps.
2. Bulletin board materials (pictures, articles, diagrams, etc.).
3. Portions of textbook supplements.
4. Vocabulary drills.
5. Projecting student work, such as a good paragraph written either for homework, a test, or creative writing for a certain unit.
6. The use of reproduced textbook pages themselves on the projector, pointing out important paragraphs, words, phrases.
7. Art study, such as Gothic, Doric, etc.
8. Newspaper articles of recent events pertaining to ancient history, especially archaeology.
9. To teach correct form of outlining.
10. To teach expressive oral reading or profitable silent reading.

Overlays Can Be Effectively Used

The overlay capability of overhead projection is as valuable in the teaching of history as in any other subject. This is vividly demonstrated by two transparencies offered by Willow Glen High School of San Jose, California.

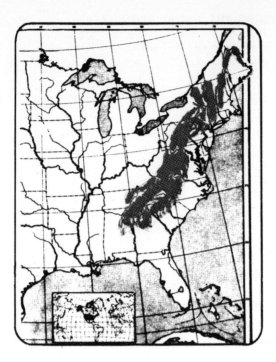

Figure 7.5. Overlays to show population growth and spread are useful in history classes.

The first of these is seen in the series of Figure 7.5. It was used in a class in early American history to show the growth of population in America during the short span of 100 years, from 1650 to 1750. It also demonstrates the growth outward of population from the seacoast over the Appalachians and to the south.

The basic transparency, merely a reproduction of an outline map of America east of the Mississippi, was reproduced onto clear direct reading image positive film. The teacher used a brown grease pencil or crayon to color in the Appalachian range.

Overlay 1, showing the population density in 1650, is hinged to the right of the mount to which the basic transparency is taped. It is composed of a series of small dots to show the density of population at the time.

Overlay 2, showing the growth and movement of population in 1750, is hinged to the left of the mount to which the basic transparency is taped. It, too, is composed of a series of dots.

The second demonstration of overlay as it applies to the teaching of history is more sophisticated, especially in its use of color to define clearly points of historical fact the teacher wishes to make. It is composed of a basic transparency and three overlays, all of which are prepared in free-hand by the teacher to show the makeup of Europe in 1812, at the height of Napoleonic power (Figure 7.6).

Figure 7.6. What better way to show opposing and allied nations during a period in history than by the use of overlays.

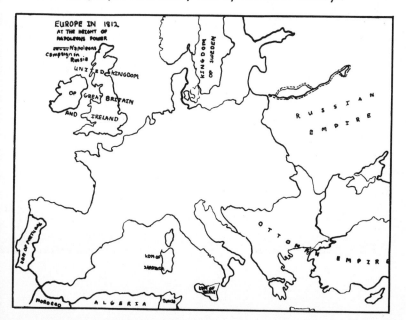

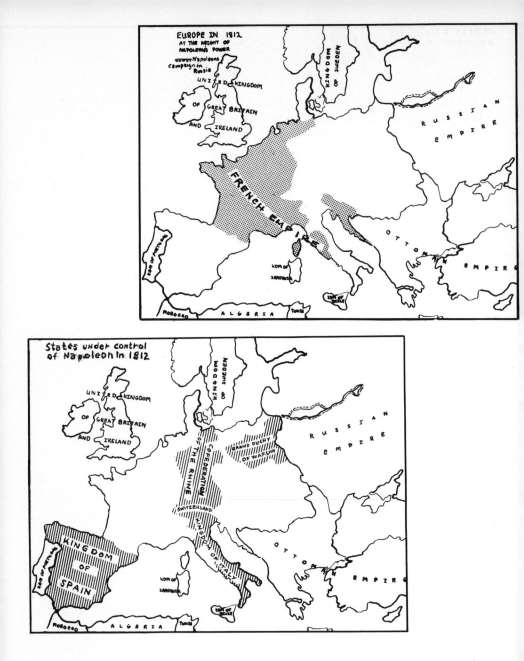

The basic overlay is a free-hand map of Europe and shows those countries not in concert with, but opposed to, Napoleon. No color is used. Instead, the map is reproduced onto direct reading image positive film.

Overlay 1, hinged to the right of the basic transparency mount, shows the French Empire in proper registration with its position in the basic

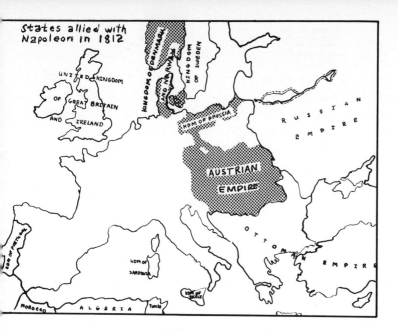

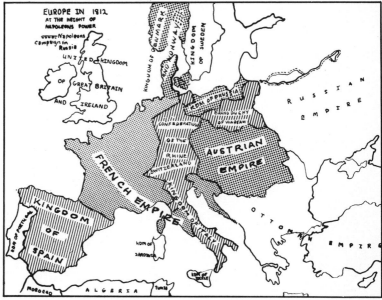

transparency. After being reproduced onto clear direct reading image positive film, it is colored in blue.

Overlay 2, hinged to the top of the basic transparency mount, shows those states of Europe under control of Napoleon in 1812. It is prepared in the same manner as overlay 1, but is colored in red.

Finally, *Overlay 3*, which is hinged to the bottom of the basic transparency mount, shows those states allied with Napoleon. It, too, is prepared in the same manner as the others, but is colored in green.

When put together and projected, students are able to see at a glance the four divisions of Europe which the teacher wants them to see—the French Empire, those states under Napoleonic rule, those states allied with Napoleon, and those states opposed to him.

Use of Projection in College History Summarized

On a college level which, as you will note, is not too different from elementary and high school levels in its use of the equipment, overhead projection can be widely employed to teach history. An excellent dissertation concerning this employment has been offered by Moorhead State College of Moorhead, Minnesota. Parts of this discussion are presented here for your edification.

Moorhead's history department has established a minimal and maximal program for projection. The minimal program deals with the ordinary classroom situation and demonstrates the projector's potential as a medium in mass instruction. The maximal program deals with use of the projector in the history laboratory.

In the minimal program, three uses of the projector are proposed. The first is that of maps. This is what Moorhead State College's history department says about this area:

> Classroom maps made by American suppliers are absurdly small for history classes. European maps are larger and better, but cost too much. All maps—whether American or foreign—are years behind the times in presenting the new concepts of history worked out by pioneers in hitherto neglected sub-disciplines such as the history of technology, the history of religion, etc., and by A. J. Toynbee and his followers and critics. We propose to make transparencies of the best European and American maps, and of maps prepared by ourselves. They will be projected on the largest scale possible.

In the area of diagrams, Moorhead College's history department has a special interest to offset weaknesses of the past. This interest is summarized as follows:

> ..... We would make transparencies of our own, based upon our own material and ideas. We have tried to present these ideas on the blackboard, but few professors can draw well. When we are not gifted that way, we will have transparencies of diagrams

prepared well in advance of class, making use of an artist. Previously, the awkwardness of other transparency systems has dampened our enthusiasm for this approach, but modern projection systems seem to meet all reasonable objections.

The area of special historical illustrations also plays an important part in the minimal requirements established by Moorhead's history department. Here is what this department has to say about this area:

> In history we often need to reproduce and exhibit to the class an unusual or rare picture of one thing or another: pages from manuscripts, newspaper cartoons, sections of very old books or documents, and so on. Considering the apparent ease of reproducing such items with overhead projection equipment, we expect that our use of these will soon come to be a large part of regular classroom effort.

Something entirely new and perhaps revolutionary in historical learning has been proposed at Moorhead. It is based on the use of the overhead projector and, were it not for the availability of this equipment, could not otherwise be considered. The essence of the proposal concerns the establishment of a history laboratory. The laboratory would be equipped with one projector and a reproduction device and "will attempt new techniques in the use of visual images in studying the past."

One area which illustrates the use of the laboratory is that of research papers based on non-written historical materials. The following is the highlight of the proposal made by this department:

> It is a fallacy that history is written or based on written records only, but owing to the great cost of illustrative materials the teaching of history has stressed the printed word.
>
> We regularly assign term papers to students who are directed to go to the library and cull information from a certain collection of books (those pertaining to economic history, let us say). What we now propose is that a laboratory be set up wherein transparency sequences in the various sub-fields of history are set out, and where students will be directed (or allowed) to go to view a sequence of transparencies pertaining to the subject on which they propose to make a report.
>
> Sequences will have been prepared by the department long in advance, naturally. Ultimately, each of our courses might have its own sequence. A trained student assistant would be on duty to project the images at a rate of speed which allows the student

to gain a real understanding of the meaning of what he sees. Students would sign up for certain hours of projection during the terms, just as science students sign up for turns at laboratory equipment in that field of learning, or as happens in libraries where students check out reserved books. In short, the student who elects to do a term paper on *visual* material could go to the history laboratory and do almost all of his research there. We may of course require some special reading as an aid to the project, but for that reason only.

Moorhead's history department then asks the question," Is the laboratory idea a frill or a necessity?" And they answer it in a most effective manner:

Everyone knows that reliance on reading alone has been killing interest in the subject. Students are assigned to look at illustrative books which the library might have on hand, and professors keep a sharp eye for cheap illustrated books that each student might purchase for himself along with the text.

These methods have proved disappointing. Illustrative books are more expensive every day, and only the finest libraries have a large number of them. Few have enough to cover the entire span of man's past. Furthermore, courses vary from college to college and a handbook made for a certain kind of class has a way of getting badly out of date with each new archaeological or conceptual advance in the discipline. Books on the first civilizations are notorious for this.

Finally, the whole attitude of historians is changing, and so far there is no agreement as to where curriculum reform will end. At Moorhead we start the freshman major on a two year course of comparative civilization (using the Toynbee list). This is a very unusual approach and we know of no cheap or halfway-complete set of illustrations that would be of any use to it. But on our own we can put together numerous illustrations from diverse sources and make up a sound sequence of transparencies which illustrates all the points we wish to make. After all, teachers differ. Why not exploit the differences!

The basic idea we are presenting . . . is the writing of term papers from the materials thus collected and presented. To merely ask (or require) history students to enter a room and look at so many images during a given quarter or semester would produce little learning, in most cases. But if students are told that they must explain *what they see,* and *write it up,* citing transparencies in the same way that they would cite library books in an ordinary research paper, they will have to force themselves to master the self-study of images—a technique that has to be learned. It amounts to meditation, in plain language, and meditation is not congenial to Western man. But once it was. We can recapture the art, if we try. The most doltish peasant in medieval times was prepared to draw endless conclusions from a stained-glass window. There is no need to send students to Europe or India for this purpose. It can be done in a laboratory.

How to Employ Projection
to Teach Other Social Sciences

Teachers who are responsible for instructing students in the other disciplines of the social sciences, specifically geography and political science (or current events, civics, problems of democracy), put as much stress in overhead projection as a teaching aid as other teachers instructing on other courses. The following demonstrate how your colleagues are using overhead projection in teaching their classes.

Again, the concept that "one picture is worth 10,000 words" is demonstrated in the types of transparencies available for projection in a course in geography. Vocabulary is vital; there is no substitute for terms, and each student must know and understand words. What better aid is there to the teaching of terms than overhead projection?

Take the terms "parallel" and "meridian," for example, as did teachers at Fontana High School in Fontana, California. Only one transparency (Figure 7.7) was needed to bring the terms and their meanings

Figure 7.7. Can words convey the meaning of the terms "parallel" and "meridian" as effectively as does this projection?

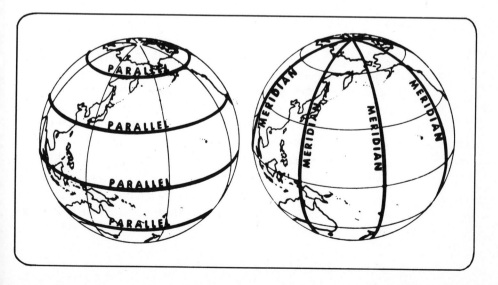

Figure 7.8a. This is the basic transparency used in a geography course to teach terms.

clearly into perspective. And a simple transparency it is, being a reproduction of a page from a book that the teacher had in his possession.

Another representative example of how overhead projection is used to teach geographical terms is demonstrated by teachers at Genesee-Humboldt Junior High School in Buffalo, New York. The method makes use of one transparency.

The basic transparency, mounted in a frame, is a free-hand drawing of a peninsula and surrounding area (Figure 7.8a). It is reproduced onto clear direct reading image positive film. If the teacher desires, areas can be colored by means of crayon or colored grease pencils.

The overlay contains the names used for the peninsula area (Figure 7.8b). The terms are in correct registration with the basic transparency. When projected, each term, of course, is discussed as to meaning.

Why did the teacher make an overlay when she could have used just one transparency employing both illustrative matter and terms? The answer to this lies in her desire to make the greatest use of the transparency possible. In this case, it was used as a quizzing device.

After terms have been learned, the overlay transparency is removed and a clear sheet of unexposed transparency film is placed over the basic transparency. A grease pencil is laid on the projector. The name of the game is called, "I know a place which is —————." It works like this.

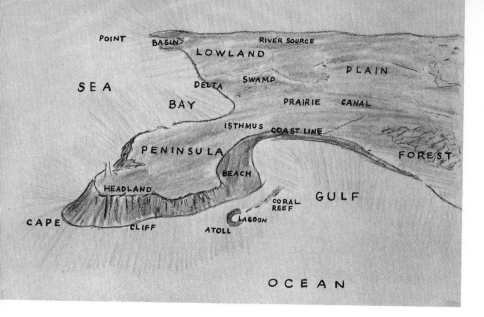

Figure 7.8b. This is the overlay used with Figure 7.8a. It contains, in proper registration to that figure, the terms which the teacher wants learned.

A student leader asks, "I know a place which is a delta. John, do you?"

John goes to the projector and writes in "delta" where he thinks a delta is.

"Is he right or wrong?" the student leader asks, and other students are called upon to place "delta" where they believe the delta is if they disagree. It is left to the student leader to determine the accuracy of one of the answers or the inaccuracy of all. If he is wrong, another student replaces him as leader.

Finally, terms can be understood, especially in the lower grades, if students actually see what the regions described by the terms look like. For example, elementary students at Sunset Elementary School in Selah, Washington, are asked, "What is a desert?"

Actual pictures of a desert, reproduced onto color lift transparent film so a true representation is achieved, are projected. There are numerous pictures of desert regions continually printed in full color in magazines, as there are of other geographical regions, such as polar areas, jungle regions, mountain ranges, valleys, and so forth.

Learning National Geography by Overhead

Maximum advantage can be made of overhead projection in the area

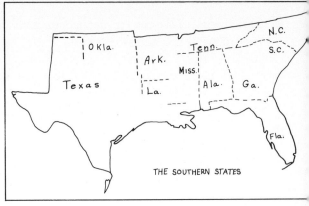

Figure 7.9a. This forms the basic transparency used in a geographical course on the southern states of the United States.

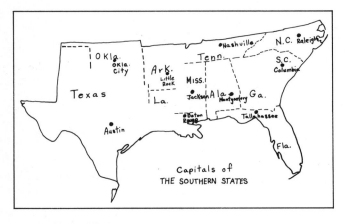

Figure 7.9b. Overlay 1, in proper registration with Figure 7.9a, shows the capital cities.

Figure 7.9c. Overlay 2, in proper registration with Figures 7.9a and 7.9b, shows the river systems.

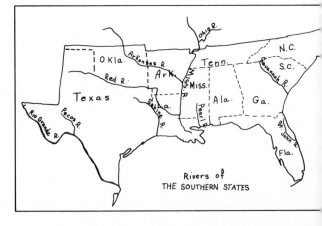

of map studies. This can be applied to both countries and sections of countries. Let us cite one example.

At Maple Ridge Elementary School in Somerset, Pennsylvania, the projector is used in fifth grade classes to study different sections of the United States. Overlay is employed.

A basic transparency is prepared of a section of the country and mounted in a frame. Overlay transparencies are then made of capitals, rivers, mountain ranges, industrial centers, land elevations, or what have you. Each transparency is colored in a different color with crayon, grease pencil or felt marker.

For example, in a study of the southern states of the United States, a basic transparency is made of these states (Figure 7.9a). Two overlays are then prepared, one to show the capital cities (Figure 7.9b) and one showing the river systems (Figure 7.9c).

Overhead projection can be used in a similar manner as it is used in history and geography to study current events and political science. Reproductions of newspaper clippings, pictures of leaders from magazines, maps to show new and old boundaries or the progress of wars, charts and diagrams to show responsibilities of governmental organizations, and checks and balances—these and many more can be employed effectively.

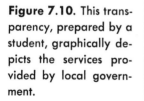

Figure 7.10. This transparency, prepared by a student, graphically depicts the services provided by local government.

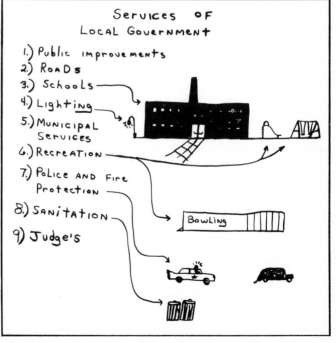

As one example, let us cite a presentation made at Eastlake Junior High School in Willoughby, Ohio. The course of study concerned local government. These transparencies are offered:

Figure 7.10 shows how the teacher had *a student* portray the services provided by local government by letting him prepare a transparency.

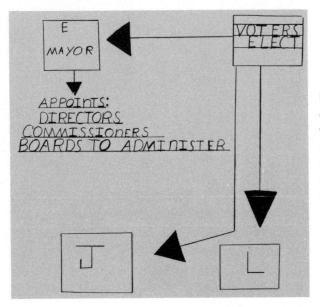

Figure 7.11. A simple diagram, projected on the screen, tells students at a glance who the people elect on the local level and who are appointed.

Figure 7.12. Understanding the mayor-council form of government is difficult because of its complexity. When used in a lecture, this diagram made on transparency material makes learning easier.

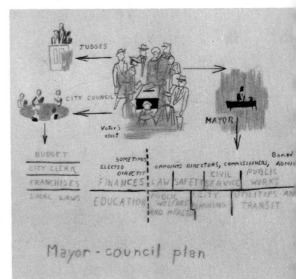

Figure 7.11 shows the electoral-appointee process on the local level. Finally, Figure 7.12 provides the basis for a discussion of the mayor-council form of local government. All are effective and enabled students to learn rapidly and retain more of what they learned because they could *see* it—they didn't have to mentally visualize the subject matter.

8.

Use of the Overhead Projector
in the Teaching of Foreign Languages

Many teachers of foreign languages agree that there is nothing more foreign to American students than foreign languages. Students in other lands seem to possess a greater ability to learn a language other than their own. Not so with American youngsters, who seem to have a mental block to French, Spanish, German, et al. And when it comes to Greek and Latin—well, they look upon Greek as if it were Latin, and upon Latin as if it were Greek.

This obstacle to accepting, understanding, and speaking foreign languages makes the job of the foreign language teacher that much more difficult. In the past, the teacher would compound drill upon drill, trying to pound into the minds and mouths of the students the language she was teaching. It cannot honestly be stated that overhead projection will do away with this and remove the mental obstacles presented to students by foreign languages. But it can and has helped.

The objectives of the foreign language teacher in today's audio-lingual-visual classroom are in this order, comprehension, speaking, reading, and writing of the target language. Since a considerable amount of time must be given to understanding and speaking the new language before the written word (or symbol) is introduced, "pictures" become vitally important as the bond between the known and the unknown. These "pictures" can be placed on transparencies and filed according to lesson or subject so they are readily available to teacher and class.

In the choice of pictures, the teacher should be guided by two simple principles, as follows:

1. Situations are more important than words.
2. New vocabulary should be embodied in the situational concept.

The remainder of this chapter depicts these principles in action as demonstrated by the way in which language teachers across the nation are making use of "pictures"—that is, the visual aspects of teaching language—in their everyday presentations.

Projection Used for Manuscript Studies

In the Middlesex School's (Concord, Massachusetts) Latin program, considerable emphasis is placed upon manuscript study, especially where the validity of an ancient text is concerned. "Very often, individual words in the texts, occasionally entire passages, are under dispute by classical scholars," the teacher states. "The text being used by a given class, reflecting as it does the opinion of its editor alone, is in effect a one-sided representation of the scholarship that has been devoted to the piece of literature involved. It is the teacher's task to provide his class with texts presenting the other side."

However, this is a major task since it involves the searching out of such texts and their eventual application to mimeograph sheets. It requires an amount of time disproportionate to the total number of classroom hours spent on such projects.

"But worse than that," the teacher exclaims, "time forces the mimeographing of only one contrary version of the text, where in fact several may exist; thus the original problem has not been solved at all."

The Latin teachers at Middlesex have found, however, that the necessary number of disputed texts can be copied for permanent use on transparent material. By using several overhead projectors side by side, several versions of a text can be projected against the classroom wall at the same time, dramatizing the differences.

These teachers of Latin find another valuable use for projection. According to them, "although there is no shortage of books that carry examples of original Latin script, the intricacies of the script make it impossible for a teacher to reproduce it on a stencil. The teacher is forced to pass around the book or a single sheet. This is at best an inefficient process."

However, by using projected transparencies an interesting alternative is proposed. Examples of original Latin script are reproduced and presented. The teachers use felt markers to color the transparency, which restores to the image at least some of the illumination of the original.

Teaching Paleography by Projection

The science of paleography—deciphering ancient writings—is being offered in Latin classes at Middlesex in a much more dramatic and efficient way than the method previously used, which was chalkboard. This science, which seems to hold a fascination for students of Latin, is made more interesting, while at the same time contributing to the students' understanding of the language.

Since paleographers reconstruct inscriptions as they originally appeared from a few letters, students are encouraged to decipher or

Figure 8.1. Paleography, the science of deciphering fragmentary bits of ancient writing, can now be introduced into the classroom as a direct result of overhead projection.

complete fragmentary inscriptions copied onto transparencies (Figure 8.1). After the students try their hand, the teacher places an overlay over the basic transparency. The overlay shows the inscription as completed by paleographers.

"In such a way," the teachers suggest, "more paleographic studies can be presented in a shorter time, and the method of presentation is dramatic enough to insure full class participation."

Composition Methods Developed

Just as in classes devoted to English composition, the overhead projector can be used in language studies to stimulate class participation

Figure 8.2. A student composition, reproduced onto transparent material and projected, invites full class participation in making corrections and discussing the work in the language being studied.

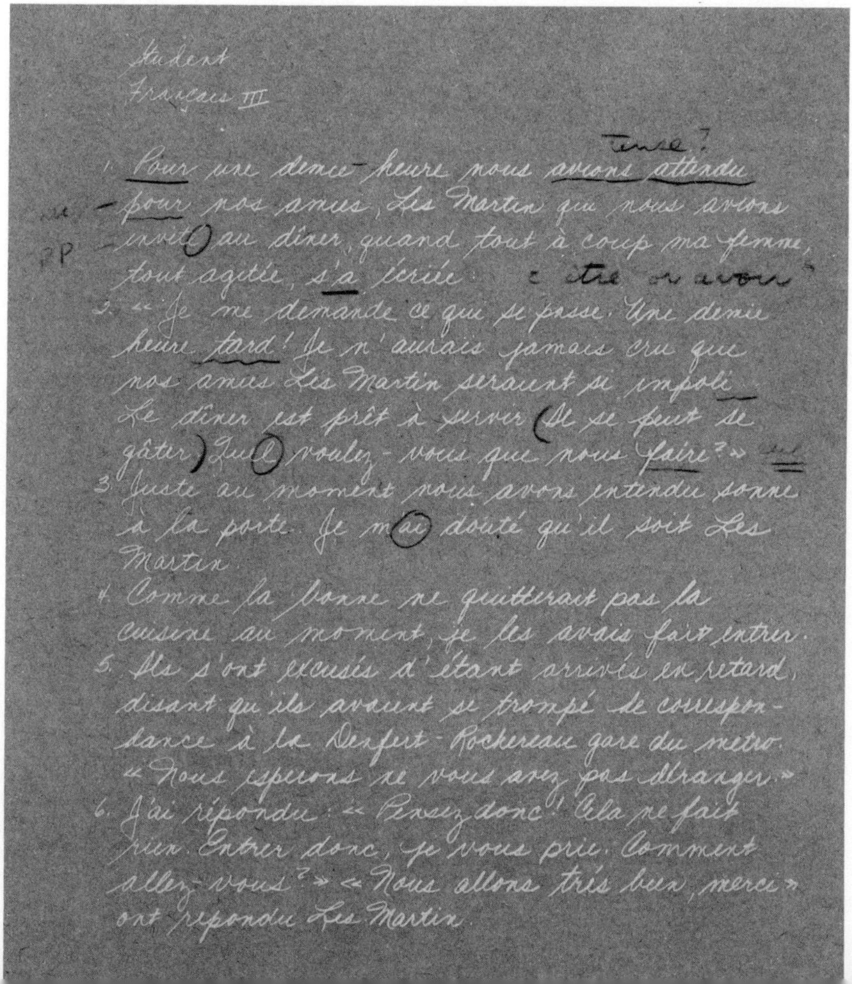

Student
Français III

tense?

1. Pour une demie heure nous avons attendu pour nos amies, Les Martin qui nous avions invité au dîner, quand tout à coup ma femme, tout agitée, s'a écriée. être or avoir

2. « Je me demande ce qui se passe. Une demie heure tard! Je n'aurais jamais cru que nos amies Les Martin seraient si impoli. Le dîner est prêt à servir (Il se peut se gâter) Quel voulez-vous que nous faire? »

3. Juste au moment nous avons entendu sonne à la porte. Je m'ai douté qu'il soit Les Martin.

4. Comme la bonne ne quitterait pas la cuisine au moment, je les avais fait entrer.

5. Ils s'ont excusés d'étant arrivés en retard, disant qu'ils avaient se trompé de correspondance à la Denfert-Rochereau gare du metro. « Nous espérons ne vous avez pas déranger. »

6. J'ai répondu: « Pensez donc! Cela ne fait rien. Entrer donc, je vous prie. Comment allez-vous? » « Nous allons très bien, merci » ont répondu Les Martin.

and increase their responsiveness to mistakes in grammar and word usage. This is demonstrated by a technique employed in a French composition class at Mercy High School in Baltimore, Maryland.

The composition of a student is reproduced onto direct reading image positive transparency material and projected (Figure 8.2). Students are then instructed to make corrections in grammar, read for comprehension, and suggest words other than those used which could better convey meaning.

A similar technique is used in classes devoted to Greek, but this one emphasizes Greek penmanship. The Greek alphabet is copied in two rows down the sheet of transparent material, with enough room left on the right hand side of the sheet to form another row. The transparency is projected. The teacher then goes down the rows and copies each letter with a red grease pencil (Figure 8.3). This permits the class to see and observe the hand movements used to form the letters.

The blank row on the right hand side of the transparent material is utilized for two purposes: it permits the teacher to write, in English, equivalents to the letters being demonstrated or permits her to write Greek words possessing the letters she is demonstrating.

Projection Makes Languages "Lively"

"In view of the new emphasis placed upon the teaching of foreign language in secondary schools," state the language teachers at Cheyenne Central High School in Cheyenne, Wyoming, "new approaches must be found to make language study lively and provocative. Overhead projection is invaluable to us in helping to achieve this.

"For example, since some of our language classes are overcrowded (one beginning German class has an enrollment of 33, while the ideal language class size is 15), we could be spending much time in presenting material and correcting papers. But the overhead projector is an immense help in alleviating this time problem."

The teachers at Cheyenne High make several concrete recommendations regarding several broad areas of language study. Since these might be of value to you, we present them here for your perusal.

● **1. Presenting grammar.** Traditionally, grammar is outlined on the chalkboard. While doing this, the teacher's back is to the class, thus obstructing vision and making for poorer hearing. Even if the teacher

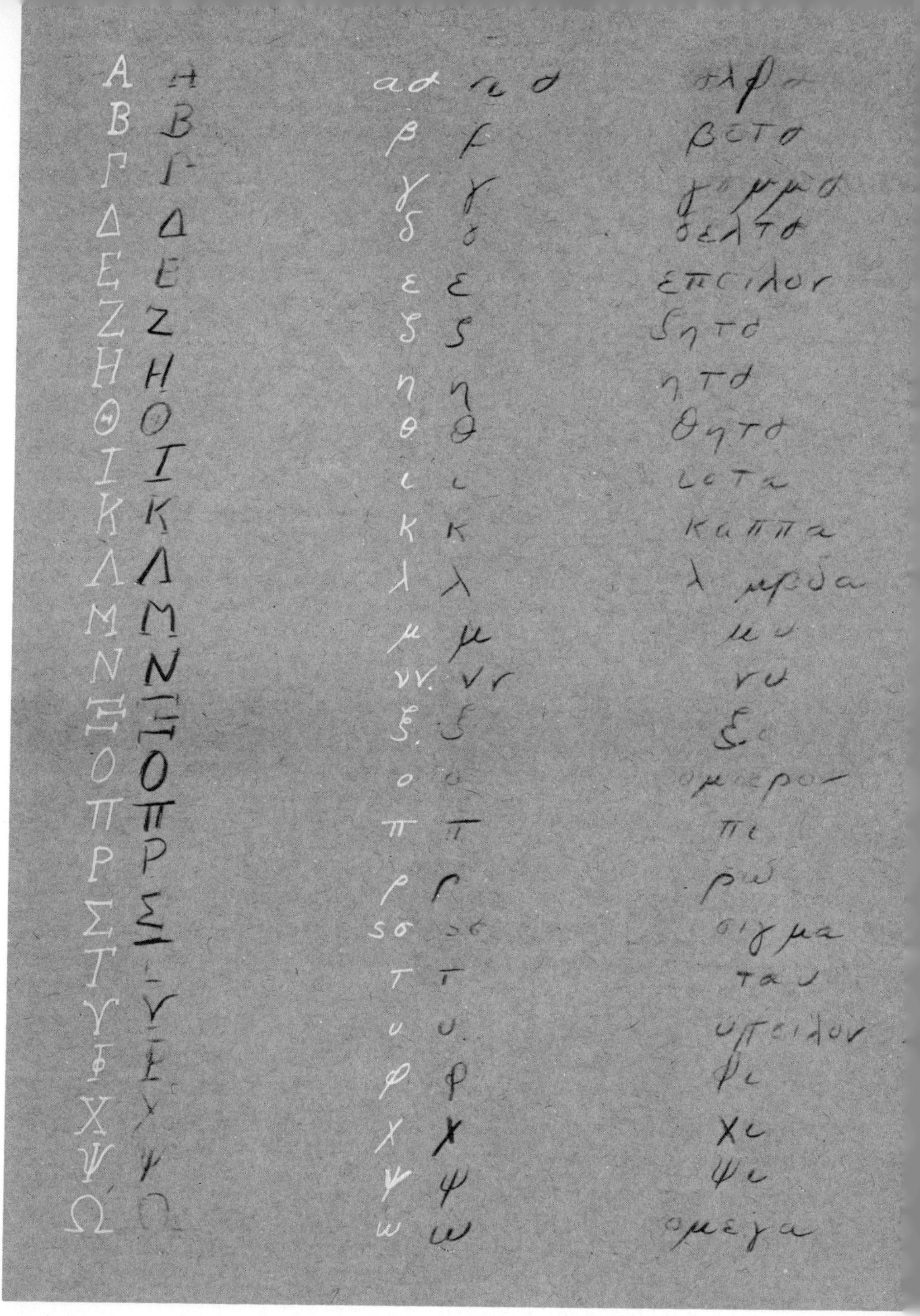

Figure 8.3. A simple transparency such as this one permits students of Greek to observe hand movements in making letter formations.

were to outline the material on the board before class, the students would be distracted by the unexplained material.

With the transparency projected on a screen, however, the teacher faces the class while explaining the material. He can explain it step by step, utilizing overlays. Every student is able to hear and see much better, especially the students in the back rows, since the projection is much larger and clearer than writing presented on the chalkboard. Also, transparencies can be used again and again for other classes.

● **2. Presenting new situations in language.** For maximum learning, classes should be conducted in the foreign language and the use of English avoided as much as possible. Thus, a diagram or a picture illustrating a new situation can be flashed on the screen which the students could grasp pictorially. They would discuss the situation in the language, without having to translate from one language to another. This method also eliminates the time-consuming explanations and makes the situation more meaningful for the student.

● **3. Testing.** Self-evaluation is particularly important, not only for motivation but for more efficient language learning. While giving a dictation the teacher can write the answer on a transparency while the class is writing. At the end of the dictation, he can turn on the projector, show the transparency, and the students can immediately determine their mastery of the material. This immediate reinforcement helps to eliminate the learning of errors and motivates the student.

Weekly quizzes, too, can be written on transparencies, thus saving teacher-time and paper. Transparencies are also more durable and easier to save than spirit masters.

● **4. Making history and geography more meaningful.** Foreign language study includes an understanding of the geography of the country in which the language is used, as well as the history of that country. The more advanced classes in particular, when studying literature, should realize the influence of the times upon the language and culture.

In the case of the German language, for example, several dialects are spoken in various parts of Germany, Switzerland, and Austria. A map with dialectical peculiarities marked in the specific areas can be flashed on the screen, enabling the students to see where these dialects occur and, hopefully, aid him in understanding why.

To illustrate the nature of changes in a language as, for example, old French to modern French or the sound changes from Old High German to Middle High German to Standard High German, the teacher could graphically present this on the projector transparency. For example, a poem of Walther von der Vogelweide, printed in Standard High German in a current text, can be presented via the projector in its original Middle High Form, which would enhance the study of both the poem and the language.

Because of the destruction of publishing houses during the war, many German and French authors are currently out of print. Short excerpts from these authors' works can be transferred to a transparency. Thus, much fascinating and educationally beneficial material, which the students otherwise might not have occasion to meet, could be made available.

• ***5. Promoting cultural understanding.*** A teacher can speak for hours about architecture, art, national dress, customs, and landscape, but nothing can match a visual approach to these areas. There are many pictures depicting these areas for all countries, but most are too small in size for the class to see as a whole and passing them around would take too much time. If these pictures are copied and projected, the

Figure 8.4. This business form in the language of the country is invaluable as a study aid to students who expect to join companies dealing with the respective country.

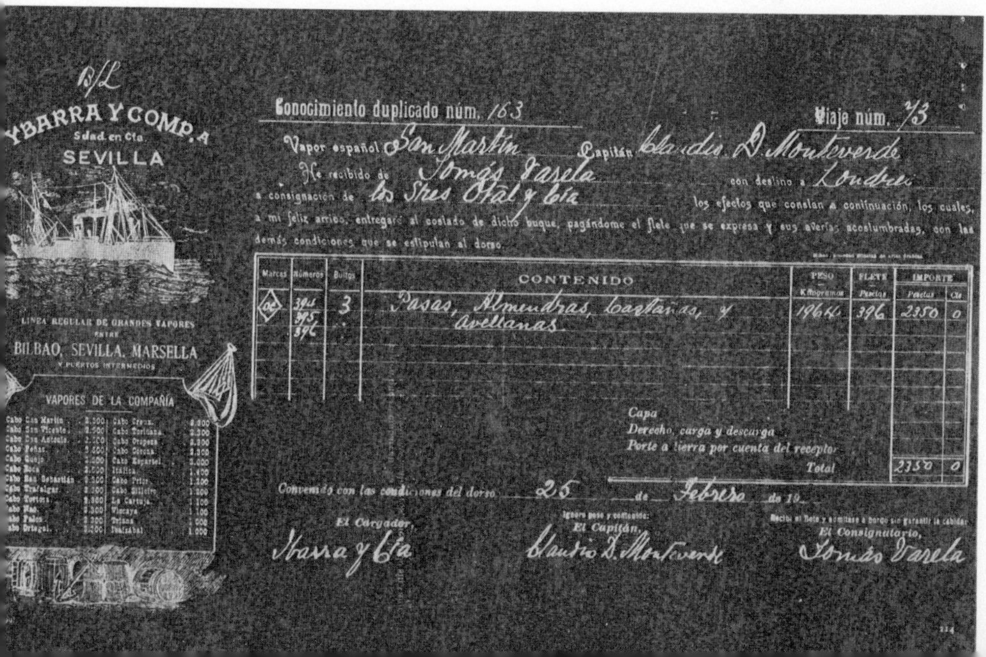

B/L

YBARRA Y COMP.A
Sdad. en Cta.
SEVILLA

LINEA REGULAR DE GRANDES VAPORES ENTRE BILBAO, SEVILLA, MARSELLA Y PUERTOS INTERMEDIOS

VAPORES DE LA COMPAÑIA

Conocimiento duplicado núm. 163 — Viaje núm. 73

Vapor español San Martín — Capitán Claudio D. Monteverde

He recibido de Tomás Varela — con destino a Londres

a consignación de los Sres Otal y Cía — los efectos que constan a continuación, los cuales, a mi feliz arribo, entregaré al costado de dicho buque, pagándome el flete que se expresa y sus averías acostumbradas, con las demás condiciones que se estipulan al dorso.

Marcas	Números	Bultos	CONTENIDO	PESO Kilogramos	FLETE Pesetas	IMPORTE Pesetas	Cts
OC	394 395 396	3	Pasas, Almendras, Castañas, y Avellanas	1964	396	2350	0
			Capa				
			Derecho, carga y descarga				
			Porte a tierra por cuenta del receptor				
			Total			2350	0

Convenido con las condiciones del dorso 25 de Febrero de 19

El Cargador, Ybarra y Cía — El Capitán, Claudio D. Monteverde — El Consignatario, Tomás Varela entire group can see them and the teacher can explain their meaning without trouble.

Teaching Business Language

Being in geographic proximity to New York, Newark, Trenton, and Philadelphia, where much of the business world conducts its operations with foreign lands, Franklin High School of Somerset, New Jersey, offers an unusual opportunity to its students. The transparency seen in Figure 8.4, which is used in a third-year level commercial Spanish course, is an example.

Such things as foreign invoices, bills of lading, and receipts are borrowed from business and made into transparencies for study and use by classes. In this way, terminal students and those bound for secretarial schools to fill positions in nearby business centers are made thoroughly familiar with what they will be facing and how to handle it—in the language required.

Learning Word Endings by Projection

"Via class lecture," a Latin teacher at St. James High School in Grand Forks, North Dakota, states, "the fact that Latin is a language of endings is explained to the students. The position of words in a sentence is comparatively unimportant because case endings of a word always identify its use in the sentence. My technique is to use color to emphasize the case (and therefore its use) of a Latin word. Because case is developed gradually, association of color and case can also develop gradually. The value of this technique can be appreciated when all the cases of all five declensions have been learned, and they are all used in composition or literature.

"Nouns of each declension, for example, can be introduced by reproducing them on a transparency and using grease pencils of different colors to emphasize endings. The transparencies can also be used for review work. This tool for teaching grammar is invaluable to me because it eliminates the repetitious writing of paradigms on the chalkboard, in the process of which I always manage to become more covered with chalk than does the board."

One of the most important uses of overhead projection in teaching a foreign language is in the area of word association to teach vocabulary.

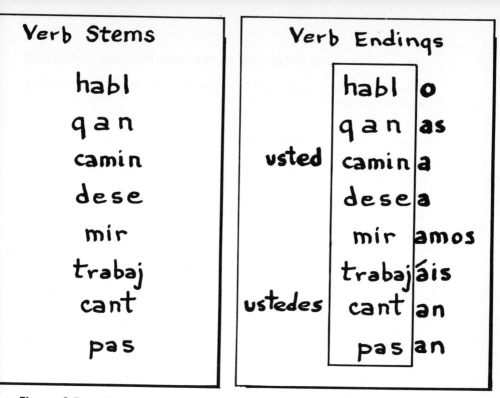

Verb Stems	Verb Endings

Verb Stems:

habl
qan
camin
dese
mir
trabaj
cant
pas

Verb Endings:

habl|o
qan|as
usted camin|a
dese|a
mir|amos
trabaj|áis
ustedes cant|an
pas|an

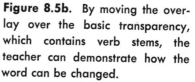

Figure 8.5a. Basic transparency and overlay can be used in teaching verb endings.

Figure 8.5b. By moving the overlay over the basic transparency, which contains verb stems, the teacher can demonstrate how the word can be changed.

"Drawings or illustrations of objects," states one teacher at William G. Enloe High School in Raleigh, North Carolina, "are transformed into transparency form and projected by me so that vocabulary can be taught by associating the word with the object, rather than by direct translation. Similarly, drawings showing types of activity help teach the meanings of verbs; arithmetic problems teach numbers; scenes teach description with vocabulary; colorful drawings illustrate colors; and so forth."

Another area of prime importance which now utilizes projection to make the learning of foreign grammar easier, and which is employed at this high school, is grammatical construction. The method makes use of movable overlays to demonstrate visually sentence structure and changes in that structure.

For example, in the teaching of Spanish grammar there is a rule that a descriptive adjective follows the noun it modifies. At Enloe High, stationary transparencies are made with several nouns written on them. Then, a movable overlay is made containing several adjectives. The latter is placed over one of the noun transparencies on the projector stage and moved from noun to noun to show variation.

This technique is similar to the one shown in Figure 8.5a and 8.5b, which is used in the teaching of verb endings. The basic overlay, the one containing the verb stems, is reproduced and mounted in a transparency mount. The second overlay, the one containing verb endings, is reproduced in black and then colored to contrast with the black of the basic transparency. In use, the overlay is placed over the basic overlay

Figure 8.6. This transparency and others like it form the basis of teaching younger students to talk in a foreign language.

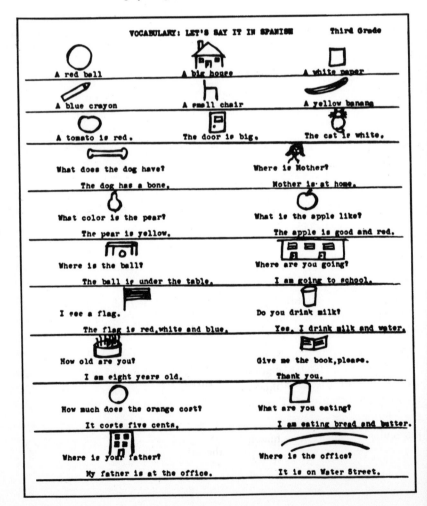

and shifted from verb stem to verb stem to demonstrate the changing of verb endings and their meanings.

Teaching Younger Students a Language

At Palm Beach Public School in Palm Beach, Florida, students are introduced to foreign languages in the third grade, and language study continues and broadens in every grade thereafter.

In the Spanish program for the third through sixth grades, the children learn by listening to the language and speaking it. They do not see or read it, and they do not have a textbook. Thus, written material must be presented in English, and much practice and repetition are necessary to learn vocabulary.

Vocabulary is taught to these younger students principally by drills and games involving the vocabulary, by stories, by conversations and dramatizations, and by correlating the Spanish with other subjects. All these devices are used in all grades and, according to the teachers using them, "the use of transparencies to us is an excellent way to present this material to the children for translation. It has immense value, especially for vocabulary review in all grades."

Figure 8.6 is just one example of how the technique is used in the third grade. The name of the game is, "Let's Say It in Spanish." The teacher prepares the original, using simple drawings to emphasize the text. It is then projected. But instead of projecting the entire transparency, which might distract the pupils, the teacher uses the revelation technique. Using plain white opaque paper, she covers that portion of the transparency not under discussion.

There is little doubt among educators that people learn a foreign language best by speaking it. Many teachers of languages demand that only the language under study be spoken in their classrooms, especially in classes on the high school and college level. To get students adapted to this method, they must start at the very beginning of their foreign language instruction.

One way to do this is emphasized by a technique used at Washington Junior High School in Seattle, Washington. Pictures and drawings are transferred to transparencies. The teacher writes a question on the transparency relating to the pictures being projected (Figure 8.7). Then the students are asked to tell all they can about the picture in the particular language.

Figure 8.7. Students can learn to speak a foreign language by observing pictures and translating what they see into that language.

Foreign songs, too, are of tremendous value in teaching the students not only the language, but also something about the culture and music of the land under study. However, teaching songs would be of limited value if it were not for the overhead projector, since it would take too long for the teacher to write the music on the chalkboard. Thus, a song (words and music) is reproduced onto a transparency and projected. Being able to see both words and music enables the students to derive maximum benefit from the lesson (Figure 8.8).

Coupling Ebacher Method with Projection

The Ebacher method of teaching a language to first and second level students is enjoying wide popularity. At St. Francis deSales High

School in Toledo, Ohio, the method is coupled with overhead projection to permit a greater coverage of material than ever before.

The teacher reproduces a page from her workbook onto transparency material. She then makes a transparency of a grid for use as a revelation device.

Figure 8.8. To learn the music of a country and also its language, songs such as this one can be projected.

Projecting the two, with the grid on top of the text, the teacher allows the students to see the text for several minutes with the English covered (Figure 8.9a). She then moves the grid to allow the English to be read (Figure 8.9b). In this way, several pages can be discussed and studied in minutes.

Figure 8.9a. The Ebacher method can be employed by means of projection. Here, the language is revealed without the English.

II

LE PÈRE MAURICE.

Germain, lui dit un jour son beau-père, il faut pourtant te décider à reprendre femme. Voilà bientôt deux ans que tu es veuf de ma fille, et ton aîné a sept ans. Tu approches de la trentaine, mon garçon, et tu sais que, passé cet âge-là, dans nos pays, un homme est réputé trop vieux pour rentrer en ménage. Tu as trois beaux enfants, et jusqu'ici ils ne nous ont point embarrassés. Ma femme et ma bru les ont soignés de leur mieux, et les ont aimés comme elles le devaient. Voilà Petit-Pierre quasi élevé, il pique déjà les bœufs assez gentiment; il est assez sage pour garder les bêtes au pré, et assez fort pour mener les chevaux à l'abreuvoir. Ce n'est donc pas celui-là qui nous gêne: mais les deux autres, que nous aimons pourtant, Dieu le sait, les pauvres innocents nous donnent cette année beaucoup de souci. Il te faut donc une autre femme et à moi une autre bru. Songes-y, mon garçon. Je t'ai déjà averti plusieurs fois, le temps se passe, les années ne t'attendront point. Tu dois à tes enfants et à nous autres, qui voulons que tout aille bien dans la maison, de te marier au plus tôt.

—Eh bien, mon père, répondit le gendre, si vous le voulez absolument, il faudra donc vous contenter. Mais je ne veux pas vous cacher que cela me fera beaucoup de peine, et que je n'en ai guère plus d'envie que de me noyer. On sait qui on perd et on ne sait pas qui l'on trouve. J'avais une brave femme, une belle femme, douce, courageuse, bonne à ses père et mere, bonne à son mari, bonne à ses enfants, bonne au travail, aux champs comme à la maison, adroit à l'ouvrage, bonne à tout enfin; et quand vous me l'avez donnée, quand je l'ai prise, nous n'avions pas mis dans nos conditions que je viendrais à l'oublier si j'avais le malheur de la perdre.

—C'est une justice à te rendre, mon fils, que tu as toujours écouté l'amitié

- 3 -

"Overhead projection is, to me, an invaluable device for saving time in the classroom," states a German teacher at this same high school. "It provides me with greater instruction time. In the course of a year, the time I save definitely adds up to several class periods. 'Bonus' instruction time—how wonderful!

Figure 8.9b. This shows development of the Ebacher system. Here, the English is revealed to coincide with the language.

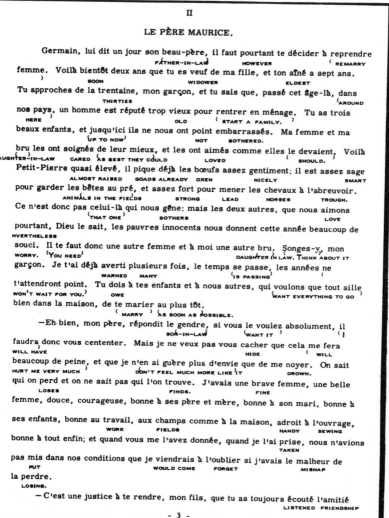

II

LE PÈRE MAURICE.

Germain, lui dit un jour son beau-père, il faut pourtant te décider à reprendre
FATHER-IN-LAW   HOWEVER   (REMARRY
femme. Voilà bientôt deux ans que tu es veuf de ma fille, et ton aîné a sept ans.
)   SOON   WIDOWER   ELDEST
Tu approches de la trentaine, mon garçon, et tu sais que, passé cet âge-là, dans
THIRTIES   (AROUND
nos pays, un homme est réputé trop vieux pour rentrer en ménage. Tu as trois
HERE   OLD   (START A FAMILY.)
beaux enfants, et jusqu'ici ils ne nous ont point embarrassés. Ma femme et ma
(UP TO NOW)   NOT   BOTHERED.
bru les ont soignés de leur mieux, et les ont aimés comme elles le devaient. Voilà
DAUGHTER-IN-LAW   CARED (AS BEST THEY COULD   LOVED   (
Petit-Pierre quasi élevé, il pique déjà les bœufs assez gentiment; il est assez sage
ALMOST RAISED   GOADS ALREADY OXEN   NICELY   SHOULD.)   SMART
pour garder les bêtes au pré, et assez fort pour mener les chevaux à l'abreuvoir.
ANIMALS IN THE FIELDS   STRONG   LEAD   HORSES   TROUGH.
Ce n'est donc pas celui-là qui nous gêne: mais les deux autres, que nous aimons
(THAT ONE)   BOTHERS   LOVE
pourtant, Dieu le sait, les pauvres innocents nous donnent cette année beaucoup de
NEVERTHELESS
souci. Il te faut donc une autre femme et à moi une autre bru. Songes-y, mon
WORRY. (YOU NEED)   DAUGHTER IN LAW. THINK ABOUT IT
garçon. Je t'ai déjà averti plusieurs fois, le temps se passe, les années ne
WARNED   MANY   (IS PASSING)   (
t'attendront point. Tu dois à tes enfants et à nous autres, qui voulons que tout aille
WON'T WAIT FOR YOU.)   OWE   (WANT EVERYTHING TO GO)
bien dans la maison, de te marier au plus tôt.
(MARRY) (AS SOON AS POSSIBLE.
—Eh bien, mon père, répondit le gendre, si vous le voulez absolument, il
SON-IN-LAW   (WANT IT)   (I
faudra donc vous contenter. Mais je ne veux pas vous cacher que cela me fera
WILL HAVE   HIDE   (WILL
beaucoup de peine, et que je n'en ai guère plus d'envie que de me noyer. On sait
HURT ME VERY MUCH)   DON'T FEEL MUCH MORE LIKE)IT   DROWN.
qui on perd et on ne sait pas qui l'on trouve. J'avais une brave femme, une belle
LOSES   FINDS.   FINE
femme, douce, courageuse, bonne à ses père et mère, bonne à son mari, bonne à
ses enfants, bonne au travail, aux champs comme à la maison, adroit à l'ouvrage,
WORK   FIELDS   HANDY   SEWING
bonne à tout enfin; et quand vous me l'avez donnée, quand je l'ai prise, nous n'avions
TAKEN
pas mis dans nos conditions que je viendrais à l'oublier si j'avais le malheur de
PUT   WOULD COME   FORGET   MISHAP
la perdre.
LOSING.
— C'est une justice à te rendre, mon fils, que tu as toujours écouté l'amitié
LISTENED FRIENDSHIP

- 3 -

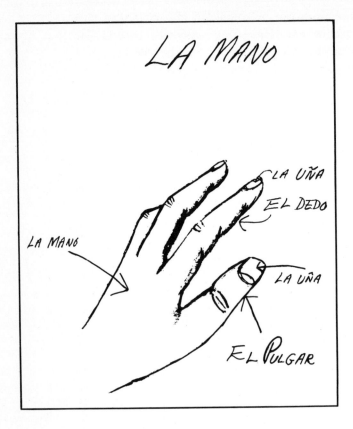

Figure 8.10. The teacher making use of this transparency insures that students will learn by association.

"For example, here are two ways in which I conserve time. I give three or four quizzes a week. It takes about five minutes to dictate the quiz or write portions of it on the blackboard. With the overhead projector, though, I flash the quiz on the screen in a matter of seconds.

"Secondly, I use the chalkboard a great deal. This takes time. However, before overhead projection, I still felt that the time had to be spent because I'm convinced that a person absorbs and retains subject matter so much better if he sees, hears, and says it. But with classroom projection I am able to display the same pertinent material I previously had to write on the chalkboard, but the time is cut to a bare minimum."

And a Latin teacher at this same high school adds her vote of confidence to projection. "Modern tests for languages," she states, "are eliminating exercise work more and more. Workbooks combine so much material that, for large numbers, a very heavy load of correcting rests on the teacher. Hours of work can be completed in a classroom in a minimum of time by having one class correct another's papers. The work sheets, returned to the original student, can be checked on a master answer sheet prepared by the teacher. The teacher, at the projector, can explain on the spot each student's problems with the various phases of the workbook lesson."

Learning by Association

We stated before that language is best learned by associating words with objects they represent. This is vividly demonstrated by the transparency seen in Figure 8.10. Simple but effective, there is no better way yet devised to learn the parts of a hand in the representative language than by this association. The same technique can, of course, be used for practically any area you can imagine. The illustration was sub-

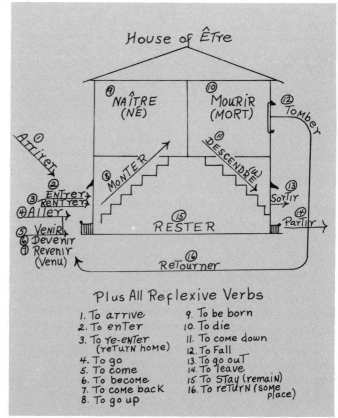

Figure 8.11. As a teacher of a foreign language, you can imagine the immense value of this transparency in teaching students a key word.

mitted by the language department of Garfield High School in Akron, Ohio.

All languages have key words, and in any language one of the most important is the verb "to be." In French, this word is "être."

At Jefferson Davis Junior High School in Hampton, Virginia, French teachers have built the "House of Être," as seen in Figure 8.11. It was built and then reproduced onto transparent material for surveillance by classes, thus providing students with a sound foundation on which to build from the base of this vital word.

9.

Use of the Overhead Projector

in Vocational Training and

the Industrial Arts

Not every secondary school student is equipped with the intelligence and money to attend college and study a profession. As in the past, the majority of these students never see the inside of a university, despite the pressure brought to bear on them that "woe will befall those who fail to seek higher education."

Are we to contend, then, that these people are "lost," being of no significant value either to themselves or society? By no means, for those who comprise the working force in industry and business are still those who have not had the benefit of higher learning. This ratio will no doubt continue into the foreseeable future, if not for all time.

The fact remains that in industry, for example, the need is assuredly great for those equipped educationally to design and develop new products for defense and consumer—those with college degrees. However, the machinist who takes an idea from the "educated" and transforms it into hardware is not, for the most part, college trained. Nor are the draftsmen who transpose the idea into detailed and readable drawings, nor the secretaries or clerks who take the clerical burden off the backs of the "thinkers," nor the telephone operators who man the communications life-line of a great economy.

It is also a fact that the majority of small and, yes, even big businessmen—the plumbers, carpenters, electricians, auto mechanics, and store keepers, for example—are not college trained.

But all these people, and others like them, *are trained* to do their specific jobs. And they get this training from the vocational and industrial arts program in secondary schools and specialized schools after high school.

Lost? Far from it. These people, indeed, continue to form the backbone of our economy, business, and perhaps the entire nation.

New Teaching Area Presented

As with other subjects discussed thus far in this book, overhead projection opens a whole new learning and teaching vista for student and teacher alike. Many schools throughout the nation have introduced projection into their vocational and industrial arts programs, and most have noticed a marked increase in student comprehension and participation.

A side benefit of projection specifically suits the vocational training teacher who travels from school to school to address audiences. This benefit is the portability and ease of operation of the projector. It is light in weight, easy to carry, and transparencies take but a small amount of room in a briefcase. The projector is set up in seconds and there is never a need for pulling shades to darken a room, since the unit can be used in a fully lighted area.

Since many of the vocational and industrial arts subjects deal with technically complicated data, overhead projection has proved invaluable from the teacher's standpoint in bringing across complex problems and facts. This will become readily apparent as you survey the examples presented in this chapter.

Let's begin simply. You know that much technical material is available from many sources other than textbooks—sources that show, for example, sketches and cross-sections of construction items. Enough copies of these are usually not obtainable to supply an entire class. And it is practically impossible, from a time standpoint, for the teacher to reproduce these by a reproduction process, such as spirit master. This material forms what is commonly called "teacher's files," and much of it is lost to the student for want of a way to introduce it.

Passing a sketch around for each student to look at takes time. Furthermore, of what benefit is it to a student to examine a complex drawing for a few seconds before he must pass it on? In addition, suppose you want to base a whole lesson on this one drawing. Is it possible for

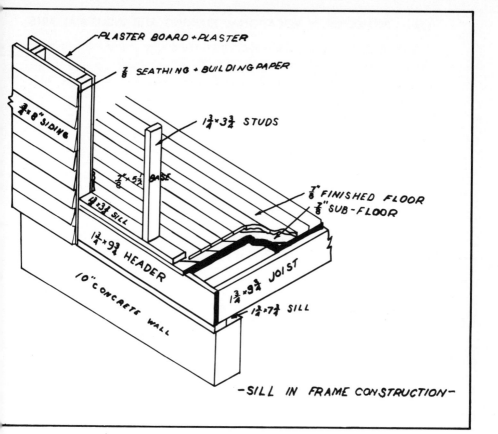

PLASTER BOARD + PLASTER

⅞ SEATHING + BUILDING PAPER

¾×8" SIDING

1¾×3¼ STUDS

⅞×5½ BASE

⅞" FINISHED FLOOR

⅞" SUB-FLOOR

1½×3¼ SILL

1¾×9¾ HEADER

1¾×9¾ JOIST

10" CONCRETE WALL

1½×7¼ SILL

—SILL IN FRAME CONSTRUCTION—

Figure 9.1. How much of this information do you think a student can retain by looking at this drawing for a few seconds as it's passed around? By comparison, with overhead projection, the transparency can be kept in full view for all to look at during an entire class period, if need be.

all students to recollect everything about a complicated drawing they have only viewed for a minute? Not likely.

But reproducing a drawing onto transparent material (just *one* reproduction completed in four seconds), projecting it by means of the overhead projector for all to see, and leaving it in full view while each important part is discussed—well, that's another matter.

A good example of this is seen in Figure 9.1, which is a transparency used in an industrial arts class at Cantrick Junior High School in Monroe, Michigan. Not only do the students see the makeup of frame construction, but they have the opportunity to associate nomenclature, so important in the trade, with object and take notes.

Range of Material Knows No Limit

"The overhead projector in the industrial arts classroom is an extremely valuable asset," states a teacher from Westlake Junior High School in Erie, Pennsylvania. "The range of material which an industrial arts instructor can use is limited only by his imagination."

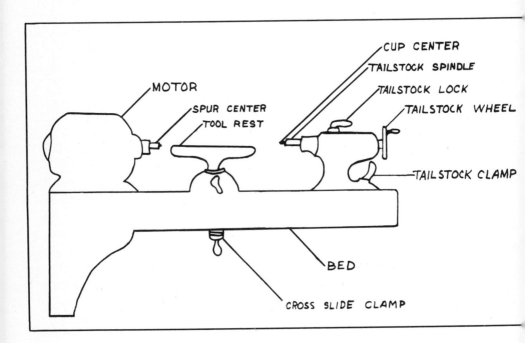

Figure 9.2. Students learn by hearing, doing, and *seeing*. This is especially true in complicated industrial art and vocational training areas.

To illustrate, this instructor submitted two transparencies which he uses. One shows the parts of a lathe (Figure 9.2), while the other shows the common wood plane (Figure 9.3).

Another transparency used at the same school is so simple in nature that anyone can prepare and make use of it, not only for vocational classes but also for classes in physics. Although simple, the information the transparency conveys is complete and easy to comprehend, and offers much more educational value than a lecture. Let us put it this way:

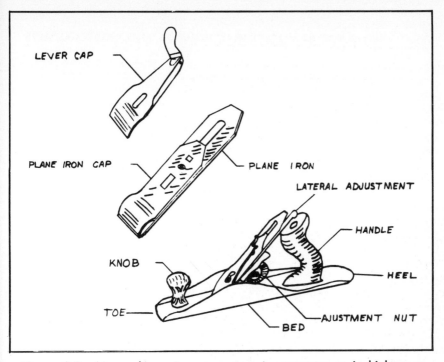

Figure 9.3. Nomenclature is as necessary in carpentry as in biology or physics. Transparencies make it easy for students to associate name with part.

How long would it take you to explain the functioning of the external combustion engine and the internal combustion engine, and the differences between the two, to a class? Now, take a look at Figure 9.4a, and you can determine for yourself the value of this one transparency.

The transparency is teacher-drawn, and, as you can see, no teacher has to be a great artist to make his own presentations. Taped to the back of the transparency mount is a piece of cardboard, which is hinged to the sides (Figure 9.4b). When the teacher discusses external combustion (the steam engine), he flips the cardboard over that portion of the drawing showing the internal combustion engine, thus revealing only the top portion. Likewise, when he discusses internal combustion, he flips the cardboard over the external combustion portion. When comparing the two engines, he simply removes the cardboard so the whole projection is revealed to the class.

Projection Facilitates Drafting Instruction

Instructors of drafting at the Bellefonte Area Joint Senior High School in Bellefonte, Pennsylvania, have found that the use of transparencies

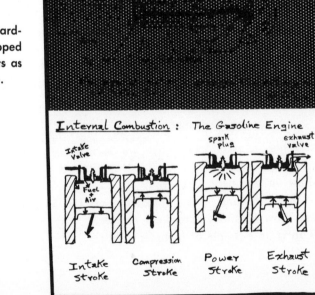

External Combustion: The Steam Engine

Steam chest
Slide Valve
Flywheel
Boiler
Fire
Connecting Rod
Crank
Crankshaft
Cylinder   Piston   Piston Rod

Reciprocal motion – changed to – rotary motion
of Piston Rod   of Fly wheel

Figure 9.4a. A simple transparency and a piece of cardboard are all that's needed to aid a teacher in lecturing about complex engine functioning.

Figure 9.4b. The cardboard, easily flipped back and forth, acts as a revelation device.

Internal Combustion: The Gasoline Engine

spark plug
exhaust valve
Intake Valve
Fuel + Air

Intake Stroke   Compression Stroke   Power Stroke   Exhaust Stroke

158

in the teaching of drafting has helped immensely the facilitation of the use of large scale drawings. Prior to projection, the teacher had the tedious and laborious task of making chalkboard drawings before each class discussion.

As you know, large scale drawings are a "must" when teaching drafting because of the frequent references made to particular parts of the drawing. Unless the teacher is able to point to that part in full view of everyone, he can never be sure that every student is aware of the part being discussed.

As one teacher in the school states, "Transparencies have not only facilitated the teaching of drafting, they have also increased the students' comprehension of the subject."

Specifically, transparencies have great value in teaching all the units of drafting instruction, particularly applied geometry, how to read the actual size scale and the proportionate scales on the architect's scale, lettering, principles of orthographic projection, sections and conventions, auxiliary views, dimensioning, and pictorial drawings.

One drafting room at this school is equipped with all of the drawing instruments and the lettering templates necessary for making custommade originals. And here's where teachers of drafting and other subjects in the school make use of student ability. Drafting students who are inclined toward illustrating abilities are encouraged to create transparencies for projection in all areas of school subject matter. And, according to a school official, these students are kept quite busy. At any time a request might come from a science, history, or English teacher to create a transparency for use in class. Quite often, the makeup and layout of the transparency is left to the drafting student, which gives him a chance to foster his creative ability.

Transparencies are also extremely useful in testing students of drafting, as Figures 9.5a and 9.5b prove. The teacher makes transparencies of Figure 9.5a for every student in the class. This involves no trouble and no great waste of time, since it takes only about five minutes to make transparencies for a class of 30. He passes these out and the students are asked to complete the transparency, showing their solution to the problem. This is easily done since it is possible to write, and draw on transparent materials.

When the time is up, students are asked to come to the projector and show what they have done, explaining why they have done it. Figure 9.5b is an example of a student answer.

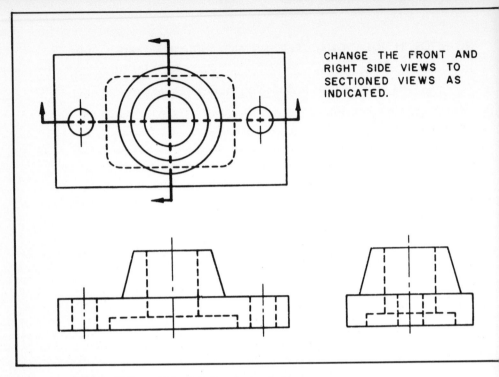

CHANGE THE FRONT AND
RIGHT SIDE VIEWS TO
SECTIONED VIEWS AS
INDICATED.

Figure 9.5a. This drawing is copied onto transparency sheets so that each student is provided with one.

Figure 9.5b. This illustration shows how one student completed the requirement called for in Figure 9.5a.

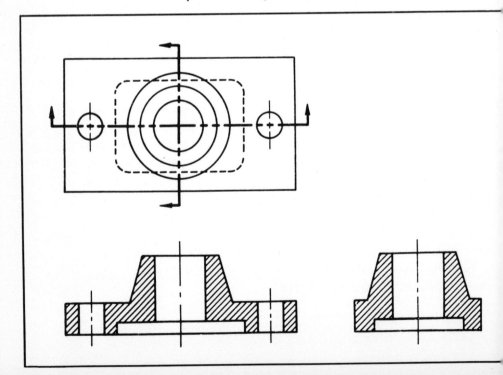

Use of Projection in Teaching Auto Mechanics

Great emphasis is being placed on mechanics to instruct those who will have the job of repairing and maintaining the nation's automobiles, trucks, and farm equipment. It appears as if school systems have listened to and taken up the challenge offered by automobile, truck and tractor manufacturers. This challenge, more in the form of a cry for help, is that there are not enough trained mechanics to service our huge and still growing (*tremendously*) "wheeled society."

Mechanics is not an easy area for secondary school students to comprehend. But overhead projection gives them every chance in the book, and most are leaving high school with a solid foundation on which to build when they begin to specialize by attending mechanic's school. Certainly, there is no better vocation a young man without a college degree can pursue than automotive mechanics. Not only does it pay well, but good mechanics are at a premium and there is a great demand for them.

At Willow Glen High School in San Jose, California, much stress is being placed on mechanics. Instructors at the school are not content, though, just to spend a year on basics. They delve into the most intricate and complex topics of all—automotive electricity and the makeup of car, truck, or tractor wiring system. Admittedly, little could be accomplished in this area without overhead projection.

Examine Figures 9.6a, 9.6b, 9.6c, and 9.6d. This is an overlay transparency. Broken down into its component parts you see the following:

1. *The basic transparency* (Figure 9.6a) shows all the electrical components, including charging system, ignition system, and accessories (lights, horn, etc.). It is reproduced from the original in black. The overlay transparencies are hinged to it, one to each edge.

2. *Overlay 1* (Figure 9.6b), a series of lines sketched in blue, shows the so-called battery circuit, and how its wires service certain areas.

3. *Overlay 2* (Figure 9.6c), a series of green lines, completes the battery circuit by showing the wiring setup to tail-lights and horn. Too much material presented in Overlay 1 would be confusing.

4. *Overlay 3* (Figure 9.6d), a series of red lines, shows the generator circuit, and the primary and secondary ignition circuits.

Certainly, these transparencies make a really complicated subject less complicated for teen-age students.

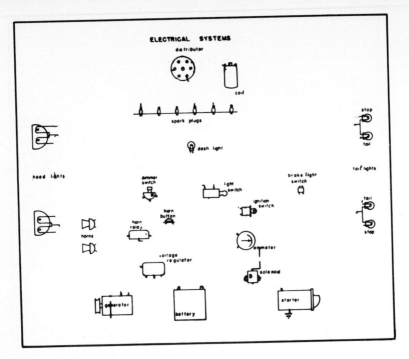

Figure 9.6a. The basic transparency shows electrical components without wiring.

Figure 9.6b. The first overlay transparency shows wiring of components that operate off the battery.

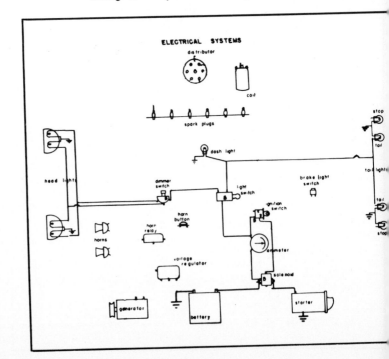

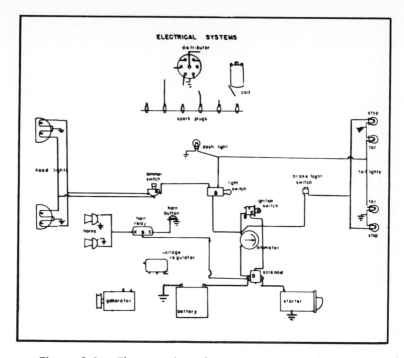

Figure 9.6c. The second overlay transparency further depicts wiring of components operating off a battery.

Figure 9.6d. The third overlay shows wiring of the generating and ignition systems.

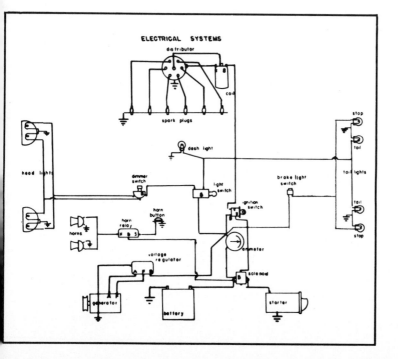

Vocational Schools Use The Overhead, Too

What does a school specifically established to teach a vocation think about overhead projection? This was answered by officials and teachers at the Fond du Lac Vocational, Technical and Adult School in Fond du Lac, Wisconsin, which devotes itself to many areas of vocational training, including machining, auto mechanics, marketing, practical nursing, and business.

One school official put it this way:

> Most adult programs are offered on a relatively short-term basis and a large variety of instructional techniques must be used to effectively stimulate learning. The effectiveness of visual education to this end has long been recognized. When the overhead projector with its wide range of uses was introduced to us, we soon learned that it was a piece of equipment which would become common to all our classrooms and all our teachers. They can't seem to get along without it.

A post high school machine shop program and apprenticeship related course in shop, and tool and die work are important parts of the curriculum at this school. The instructors that teach in this area state that there are many good books which cover machine operation and explain by picture or diagram a basic set-up or use of a machine and tools.

"As our supply of these books is often limited," they claim, "we've found that transparency material has been a source of valuable assistance in instructing. Our program also includes lists of job opportunities clipped from newspapers and other sources. These, too, lend themselves to projection since we can't buy all the newspapers we would need to go around."

The subject of perspective is of great importance to students in drafting. Figures 9.7a and 9.7b are just two transparencies borrowed from a teacher's lesson concerned with this topic. The course in which these are used is being offered at Dos Palos High School in Dos Palos, California.

As you can see, the teacher employs a bit of cartooning to "liven up" the lecture. He draws the presentation on ordinary white opaque paper, puts the original in contact with a sheet of transparent material (in this case, positive transparent material), and runs both through an infrared reproduction machine. It takes but four seconds to reproduce each transparency from its original.

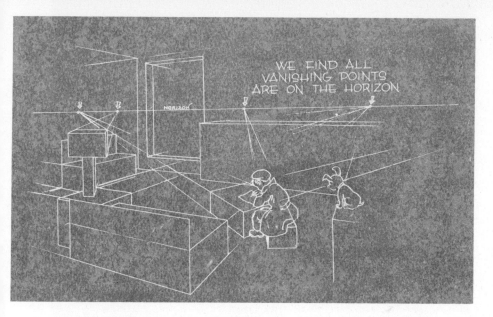

Figure 9.7a. To teach perspective, the instructor begins with a simple drawing, using cartoon characters but emphasizing principles.

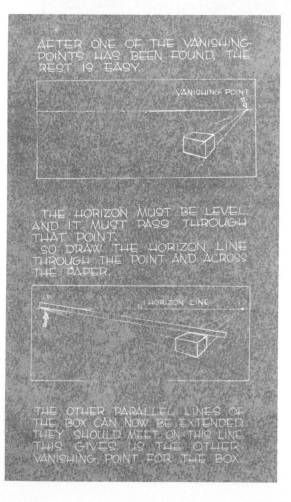

Figure 9.7b. As the lesson progresses, the subject becomes more complex, but is made easier to understand because of transparencies like this.

165

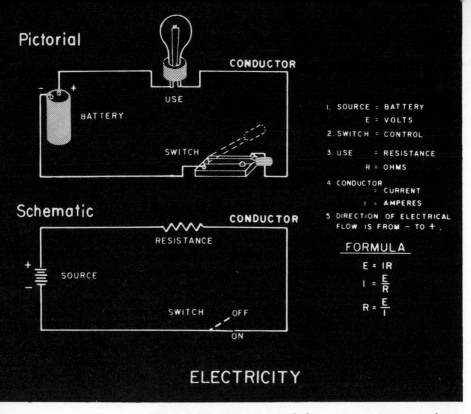

Figure 9.8. Keep in mind that a transparency made on negative transparency material and interspersed in a transparency presentation makes a refreshing change of pace.

Making Attractive Transparencies

Let us turn our attention to transparencies that are a bit more sophisticated. The ones demonstrated here are used by the Industrial Arts Department of San Francisco State College in San Francisco, California.

Being able to look at a schematic drawing and visualize a pictorial, and vice versa, is an important task for those in electronics. Furthermore, understanding the way in which electricity flows and making use of basic formulas are just as vital. To bring these points across to students, an instructor uses the transparency seen in Figure 9.8.

Although simple in makeup, the transparency is of a sophisticated nature because it is reproduced onto negative transparency material. You cannot tell by our illustration that colored transparent tape was used on the back of the transparency to make certain parts stand out. The battery in the illustration, for example, is actually outlined in red, and the bulb is outlined in yellow.

Neat, clean, simple, attractive, informative—these adjectives summarize this particular transparency.

The presentation demonstrated by Figures 9.9a through 9.9d is

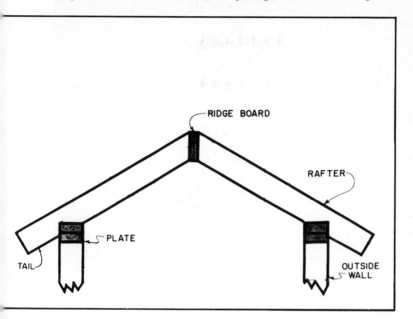

Figure 9.9a. The basic transparency in this presentation.

Figure 9.9b. Overlay 1 is colored in blue.

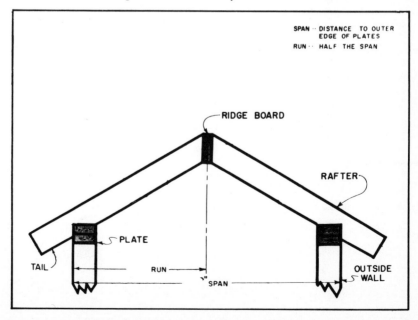

used to show students how to determine the length of rafters for a house. You can use this same idea as a basis for an excellent lesson in your class on home carpentry.

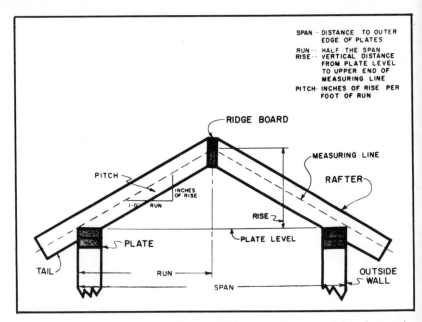

Figure 9.9c. Overlay 2 is colored in red.

Figure 9.9d. Overlay 3 completes the presentation by emphasizing formulae.

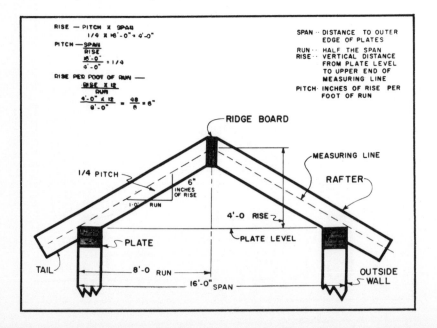

Since the points are taken in logical order, the instructor simply hinged all the overlays to one side of the transparency (Figure 9.9a). To achieve a contrast, overlay 1 was colored in blue (Figure 9.9b), overlay 2 was colored in red (Figure 9.9c), and overlay 3 (Figure 9.9d) was allowed to remain in black to blend with the basic transparency.

Projection and Sheet Metal Instruction

"In sheet metal work," states an instructor at Raleigh County Vocational Technical Center in Beckley, West Virginia, "before any job can be cut-out and fabricated, a pattern must first be developed for that specific job. To explain and demonstrate each pattern every day I used to have to resort to the blackboard and a continuous cycle of drawing and erasing in an effort to get across to students the proper methods of development. This method was not very accurate, especially

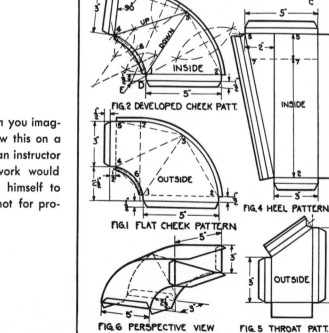

Figure 9.10. Can you imagine having to draw this on a chalkboard? Yet, an instructor in sheet metal work would have to condemn himself to this task were it not for projection.

for this exacting vocation, and was very inefficient. With the overhead projector, though, I can project each day the very complex patterns for that day, pointing out and explaining the proper steps in the development of the pattern (Figure 9.10). This permits maximum utilization of accuracy, precision and speed."

There is another advantage to employing this technique. A student drawing can easily be corrected for the benefit of an entire class by making a transparency of it, placing it on the projector, and putting the teacher's drawing, in transparency form, over it in proper registra-

Figure 9.11. Transparent colored film in a glassine envelope forms the basis of a study on photographic cropping.

tion. The two can be seen one on top of the other to reveal immediately if and when a student went wrong.

Correct cropping of a picture to add dramatic impact to that picture is an important phase of photography. Photographers and photography teachers, though, have one advantage over others in different areas of study when it comes to using the overhead projector. They often can start with a ready-made full-colored transparency, since most colored photographic film, after being developed, is transparent in nature. This obviates the need, of course, for making a reproduction onto transparent material.

For example, look at Figure 9.11, which was offered to us by a photography teacher at Reseda High School in Reseda, California. The photograph seen is in full color and is made on regular transparent photographic film. All the instructor has to do to show cropping is to slip the shot into a glassine envelope, put it on the projector, project it, and use a colored or black grease pencil to show in action how he would crop the picture for greatest impact.

Projection Used for Testing

As in other subjects, overhead projection can save the vocational teacher a great deal of time in giving a test, while at the same time providing greatest benefit to the students from that test. For example, how would you give a test on the parts of the lathe?

You would, perhaps, sketch the lathe on the chalkboard and, with call-out letters, designate the areas you want identified. Certainly, though, you would have to have some artistic ability. Or you could obtain a blank drawing of a lathe and reproduce enough copies on a spirit master machine. But how many hours would this take to get enough copies for, say, a class of 30?

Or you can use overhead projection. And to do this all you would have to secure is a picture of a lathe—easy enough. If the picture doesn't already have call-out letters on it, you sketch them in—easy enough. You paste up the original and reproduce it on to a sheet of transparency film in just four seconds, and only one copy—easy enough. You then put this one copy (Figure 9.12) on the projector and the students take the test—*easy enough*, except perhaps for those students who didn't study.

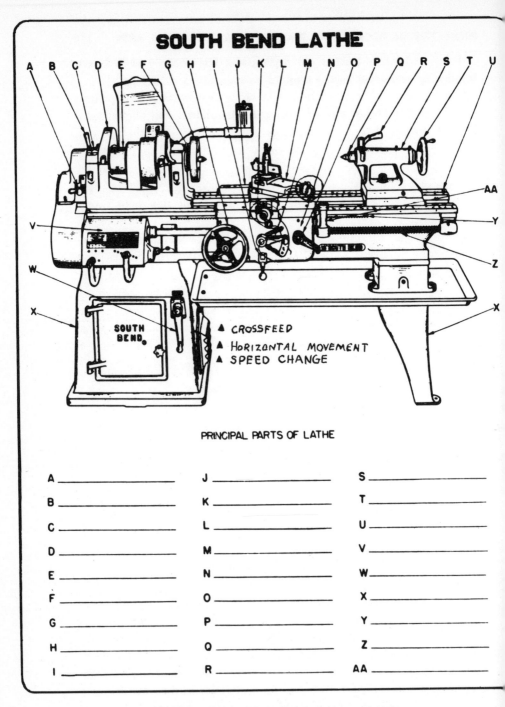

SOUTH BEND LATHE

▲ CROSSFEED
▲ HORIZONTAL MOVEMENT
▲ SPEED CHANGE

PRINCIPAL PARTS OF LATHE

A _____   J _____   S _____

B _____   K _____   T _____

C _____   L _____   U _____

D _____   M _____   V _____

E _____   N _____   W _____

F _____   O _____   X _____

G _____   P _____   Y _____

H _____   Q _____   Z _____

I _____   R _____   AA _____

Figure 9.12. This transparency was a test
given to students in machine shop work.

This is what one teacher did at Waconia High School in Waconia, Minnesota, and according to him, "it worked like a charm."

Philosophy of Projection Emphasized

The philosophy of using overhead projection in industrial arts and vocational training (and, indeed, in all other areas of education) was best summed up by two teachers in two different schools in two different parts of the country. The following is an excerpt of what one from the Judson Independent School District in Judson, Texas, had to say:

> The many advantages of utilizing the overhead projector are too numerous to list in the available space for this writing. However, if there are any deserving of primary consideration they are: (1) the ability of the teacher to always be in a position facing students while the material to be taught appears on a screen behind him; (2) the accelerated rate of learning and a higher degree of retention on the part of the students; (3) the permanency of the transparent plates and overlays for repetitive and future use; (4) the leaving of an assignment on the screen for one group while the teacher makes himself available for individual assistance to another.
>
> Industrial arts teachers in particular are indeed fortunate in having available the facilities for making their own projections. They are doubly blessed by being, as a breed, highly ingenious and accustomed to innovation. The writer enthusiastically recommends experimentation with this new medium of communication. The rewards in enriched, more interesting, and more economical presentation of the subject matter justify whatever little expense and effort are involved.

To this we must add the comments of one more instructor as he interpreted the philosophy of overhead projection. This instructor teaches at James Logan High School in Union City, California.

> In the field of industrial arts, perhaps more than any other area, proper equipment is mandatory if the student is to gain the necessary technical information. The curriculum is not only designed to instruct in certain fundamental manipulative techniques, but also to provide background and underlying theory in the various subject matter areas within the industrial arts department.
>
> Specialized demonstrations require special techniques in presenting the material. With the overhead projector, the teacher is able to present more technical information in a more meaningful manner, in less time, and with greater thoroughness, thereby providing more time for the student to apply theory learned in the laboratory.

I feel that overhead projection greatly enhances the teaching-learning situation, since such a machine makes it possible to:

1. provide more accurate graphical illustrations
2. save valuable time
3. present more meaningful information
4. simplify the presentation
5. instill a greater interest in the subject

10.

Use of the Overhead Projector
in Business Education

A classroom represents a study in forces—sometimes opposing each other, but most times trying to work together for a common purpose. One force is the body of students, but it is not a cumulative force. Instead, it is a force of individual entities of young people, each with a different intelligence capacity, each with a different personality, each with different problems.

The other force—the dominating one—is the teacher who tries to obtain a common plateau whereby the individual entities can be reached for the purpose of learning. If science could perfect "learning pills" there would be little need for teachers or for schools. Just pop a "second year Spanish pill," "a biology pill," "an American literature pill" into a student's mouth and he would be imbued with knowledge.

This, of course, might be ridiculous even to suggest, and heaven forbid this invention. What a loss to mankind and to individuality would be the learning process if "instant education" became a reality.

However, teachers themselves have long held that if every student could look over their shoulders as a computation was made, or a problem was worked out, or a grammatical structure was evolved, learning and teaching would be much easier. This, too, was looked upon as out of the question at one time. But not any more, for now it is possible for all students actually to "look over" a teacher's shoulder.

Overhead projection makes this ideal situation feasible, and it is far from a hindrance or a destroyer of the individual as would be the "learning pill." Overhead projection actually enhances education and individuality by giving every student, from the brightest to the slowest learner, full opportunity to learn and reach the optimum of his or her capability.

Various publishers of business education texts have recognized the tremendous value of overhead projection in the teaching of business. An increasing number of books are becoming available which have been specifically designed to have their material projected. One such work is *Visual Keys for College Accounting, Theory, and Practice* by Van Voorhis, Palmer, and Archer. It provides many pages of blank forms, for example, to facilitate classroom presentation by the teacher. This material can be made into transparency form for use in the classroom.

No matter what his field of endeavor, a teacher who uses overhead projection in the classroom soon begins to list, mentally or otherwise, the ways in which this valuable visual aids tool assists him. For example, the teachers of business education of the Dayton Joint High School in Dayton, Pennsylvania, have composed a list of 16 ways in which overhead projection is "of particular value to our department." In scanning this list, one immediately notices that the values do not apply only to business education. They apply equally as well to all subject areas.

Here is that list:

1. Overhead projection enables the instructor to face the students at all times.

2. The instructor has the opportunity to observe facial expressions that denote misunderstanding or lack of attention.

3. Since all material is enlarged, each student can see the material easily from his desk.

4. The teacher can use a pointer to bring important items to the attention of the class.

5. The room does not have to be darkened, which is of importance to many classrooms lacking the means of darkening a room.

6. Pictures help to make any explanation more effective.

7. The overhead projector is time saving, which is important to the student as well as to the instructor.

8. The materials can be prepared in advance, if this is desirable. Any work completed in class can be developed at a pace that is most suitable for the students.

9. The overhead projector can show printed material or handwritten material as it is developed in class.

10. Manufacturers have transparencies available which correlate with textbooks.

11. By placing one transparency on another, the actual sequence of steps in explaining the specific material can be demonstrated.

12. Material can be presented to the class at the time it will be most beneficial to them.

13. The instructor can remove, alter, cover, disclose, or complete all or part of the work at any time, or he can turn back to work previously covered.

14. The work can be done in black and white, or the teacher can prepare color transparencies to stimulate student interest.

15. Students who are slow or who for any reason fall behind in their work can be helped by repeated showing of the transparencies.

16. Transparencies can be used in the checking of homework.

Humor Aids Learning

Business education teachers at the Dayton school, as teachers everywhere, realize the value of illustrating points to imbed them in the pupil's

Figure 10.1. Cartooning and humor aid students in retention of business law principles.

A Wagering Agreement Is Unenforceable.

An Agreement That Influences a Witness in a Court Is Unenforceable.

mind. A point well illustrated is much more valuable than a point stated verbally. Words have a way of evaporating in mid-air between the teacher's mouth and the student's ear. Pictures, however, make an imprint on the eye, followed by an impression on the mind—and what is more interesting to a classroom of teen-agers than cartoons and humor.

In the teaching of business law, Dayton teachers use this approach to good advantage. They take one point and only one point, and work up a cartoon scheme. Point and cartoon are drawn on opaque paper and reproduced into transparency form for projection (Figure 10.1). Simple in makeup as these are, the illustrated points are seldom forgotten.

If the President of the United States and his learned economists have difficulty with the balance of payments problem, how can we expect students to master it? The point is that we don't expect solutions from teen-agers, but we can expect an understanding of fundamentals and, once these are learned, perhaps some fairly heady theorization.

This difficult subject—called "A Golden Difficulty" by teachers at Eisenhower High School in Rialto, California—is made simpler for comprehension by means of overhead projection. According to the teachers who use projection to introduce students to the balance of payments problem, one advantage in using the projector lies in removing much of the complexity of economic terms by means of visual contact.

Furthermore, these teachers suggest, projection "provides the teacher with a means of introducing related problems—problems such as the tariff question, gold and exchange currency deficits, foreign aid expenditures in perspective with other expenditures, and the economic effects of military commitments abroad. These issues are *viewed* as interrelated factors through the use of the projector."

In using the projector, the following steps are taken:

1. The students are shown the base map projection (Figure 10.2a). This is merely an outline map of the work reproduced onto clear direct image reading positive film.

2. Overlay 1 demonstrates the factors in red which cause expenditures (outflow) of gold (Figure 10.2b). This is a sheet of direct reading image positive film which has a red background. In other words, the image area is reproduced in black onto the red transparency film.

3. Overlay 2 (reproduced onto clear direct reading image positive film) illustrates an itemized breakdown of those factors which make up outflow of gold or exchange currency (Figure 10.2c).

4. Overlay 3 illustrates the factors in green which involve an income of gold (Figure 10.2d). This is done by reproducing a black image onto

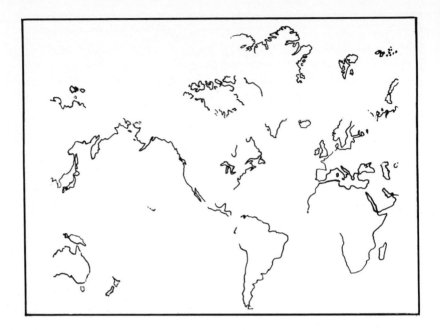

Figure 10.2a. This forms the basic transparency of the overlay scheme.

Figure 10.2b. Overlay 1 is reproduced onto transparency film having a red background.

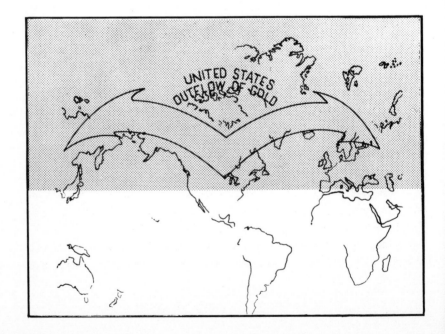

UNITED STATES
OUTFLOW OF GOLD

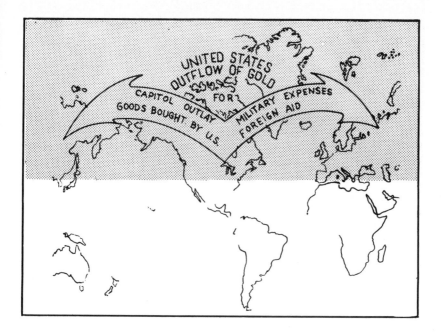

Figure 10.2c. Overlay 2 illustrates the factors involved in outflow of gold.

Figure 10.2d. Overlay 3 is reproduced onto transparency film having a green background.

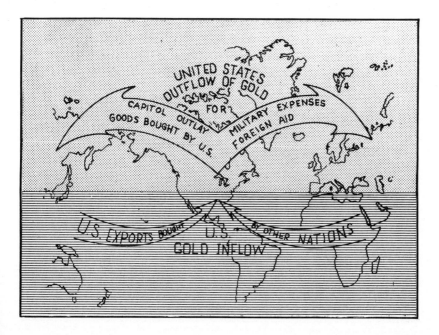

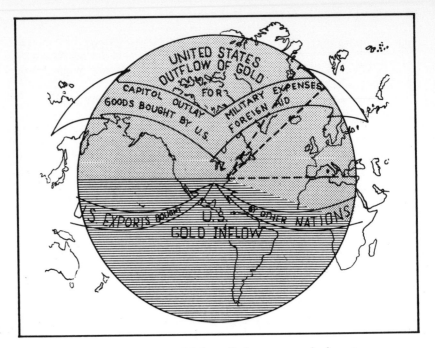

Figure 10.2e. Red, green and clear transparency material make up overlay 4.

a sheet of direct reading image positive film which has a green background.

5. Finally, overlay 4 is a circle graph (in red and green) comparing income and outflow (Figure 10.2e). When this is projected, students are asked to note the causes for expenditure or outflow of gold exceeding income. This overlay is prepared by reproducing a black circle onto a sheet of clear direct reading image positive film. Cut outs are then made from red and green transparency films and are taped in their respective positions.

Once the student has viewed the problem, and it has been explained and discussed "the teacher is in a position to pose some exciting inquiries," Eisenhower High School teachers note. These inquiries are summarized as follows:

> What are the possible solutions to the outflow of gold—i.e., deficit?
> (a) Increase exports? What are the difficulties of this solution?
> (b) Decrease imports? Difficulties?
> (c) Decrease military expenditures? What are the problems involving national security if this is done?

(d) Decrease capital investment abroad? How? What would be the effect on interest rates?

(e) Decrease foreign aid? What are the assets and liabilities of this solution?

Clearly, there is no attempt to have the teacher solve the problem for the student. The culmination of the lesson is student comprehension of a very intricate and perplexing problem.

This "exercise in thinking" would, of course, be virtually impossible to present without projection. As the teachers point out, "projection helps the student *avoid* the frequent fallacy of attempting to solve the 'gold problem' through partisan preoccupation with only one cause of the difficulty." The student is able, in short, to literally view the whole picture.

Business Letters Via Projection

Can you think of any better way to teach the writing of good business letters than by letting a class view comparison examples of good *and* bad composition and content? Probably not, but this is, at best, difficult to do without projection.

Certainly, a critique without examples would be so many words tossed through the air. And passing examples around, unless they were provided for each student, would be time consuming. Being able to give each student examples of good and bad business letters would mean much time spent by the teacher in reproducing these letters by a reproduction process such as spirit master.

But overhead projection changes all this, as teachers at Narbonne High School in Harbor City, California, prove. *One* reproduction is made of a good business letter. *One* reproduction is made of a bad letter. Both are projected, either individually or together, and *all* students see the comparison. According to these teachers, once they do, few students make the mistakes exemplified by the bad form.

At Hawley Independent High School in Hawley, Texas, the Business Department offers two years of typing, bookkeeping, and shorthand. According to teachers, "the most profitable use of the overhead projector is perhaps in the bookkeeping class. Here, the continued need for forms and reinforcement of rules in posting, journalizing, and the correct order in which to do these, brings about an essential need for repeated visionary occurrence."

Figure 10.3 shows a transparency used at Hawley High. It represents the necessity of working in a definite pattern or order of arrangement. Bookkeeping is based on knowledge of the various available possibilities with which the bookkeeper has to work in his own realm. Many firms use the same type of books, but many venture off to fit their own particular needs. However, principles remain more or less constant, and this is what this transparency endeavors to point out to students.

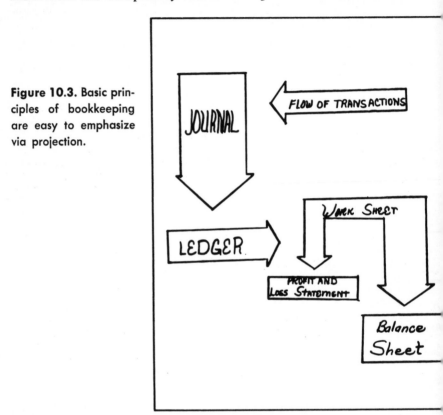

Figure 10.3. Basic principles of bookkeeping are easy to emphasize via projection.

In offering examples, Hawley business education teachers present Figure 10.4, which is a transparency of an idea on how to teach the principle of cost of goods sold. According to these teachers, "this is perhaps one of the most difficult theories to understand as well as to retain," but projection offers the means whereby it can be learned and retained.

A good example, submitted by Hawley teachers, of use in a bookkeeping class at the beginning of a year is represented by Figure 10.5.

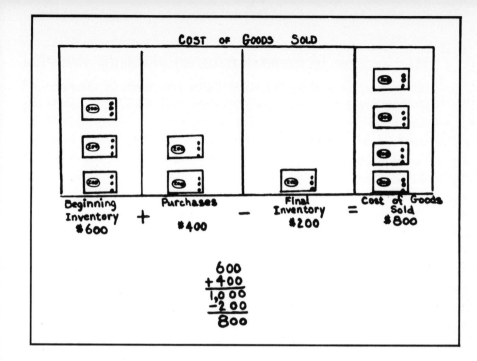

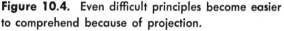

Figure 10.4. Even difficult principles become easier to comprehend because of projection.

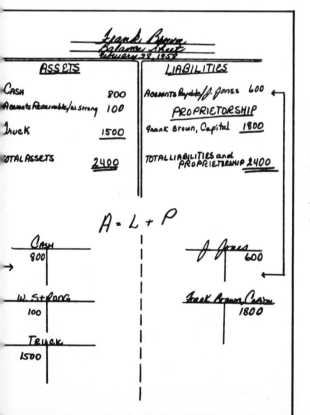

Figure 10.5. Transparencies stressing basic principles can be used throughout the year. They are permanent in nature and are not affected by light or moisture.

According to these teachers, this figure represents the basis for all bookkeeping and must be comprehended by the student.

Scope of Material Widens by Projection

Frequently, business firms send materials to teachers that would be of much benefit to the students. Unfortunately, teachers don't always have the time to duplicate such materials. However, through the use of an infrared copying machine and an overhead projector, such information as shown by Figure 10.6 can now be shared by all concerned. The transparency is being used by teachers at South Middleton Township Schools in Boiling Springs, Pennsylvania.

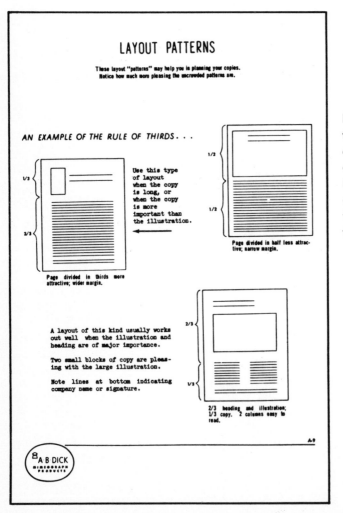

Figure 10.6. Material that the student might otherwise not have a chance to see can now be presented to him because of projection and fast reproduction of transparencies.

Classrooms for Shorthand I and II and Bookkeeping at Yreka Union High School in Yreka, California, have 8 x 8 screens that nearly eliminate the need for a chalkboard. Transparencies ruled for writing shorthand are prepared from drawn originals, and they are used to present all the shorthand theory, demonstrate penmanship techniques, and demonstrate the writing of shorthand from recorded dictation.

Special drill exercises are prepared by the instructor and developed on an infrared copying machine for repeated use. Students also correct their shorthand transcriptions from projections prepared on the copying machine or from transparencies made by typing directly on the transparency with a bulletin typewriter.

"The visual presentation of bookkeeping principles," state Yreka High teachers, "results in more recognizable advantages than are usually observable in any other class. Here, again, the instructor draws on all the forms necessary to work the same problems the student will work. After developing these forms permanently on transparencies, they are used to demonstrate all the bookkeeping steps that need to be shown.

"Usually," the teachers continue, "the instructor works the first problem on the screen at the same time it is being worked by the students. Once the students see it done correctly and have the chance to do it too, they need very little additional assistance in doing other similar problems. Another real assistance is gained from the duplication of the key and the actual projection of the detailed solutions to the assigned problems. The experience of the student in finding his own errors has far more value than the return of a teacher-corrected exercise which, in most cases, cannot properly illustrate to each student how the exercise should have been done."

Value of Projection Summarized

The value of overhead projection in a classroom devoted to business education is perhaps best summed up by the School of Business Administration of Old Dominion College in Norfolk, Virginia. Certainly, the ideas and impressions mentioned here are applicable to all schools that offer courses in this area, whether they are high schools or colleges.

The School of Business is dedicated to the concept that the most effective teaching machine ever invented is the teacher. We believe also that an excellent teacher can be more effective through wise use of audio-visual devices. Psychologists tell us that learning takes place easier, faster, and more lastingly through multi-sensory appeals. We believe that one of the best teaching aids is the overhead projector. Some of the dividends we derive from using the projector are these:

1. It provides a wide variety of illustrations, quickly and at a nominal cost, whose sources are limited only by hundreds of publications and the imagination and resourcefulness of the teacher.

2. It replaces to a large degree tedious blackboard presentations without sacrificing the element of progressive disclosure of materials. Advance preparation of materials ordinarily presented on the chalkboard saves class time and generally provides a more effective presentation.

3. It provides an excellent method of supplementing the very meager library facilities of a young, unendowed college. Through transparency projection, large numbers of students can benefit from materials, classic and current, which would otherwise be available to only a few and, in many cases, entirely unavailable.

4. It retains eye contact of the teacher with the class, which brings enormous psychological dividends. The teacher's personality is improved, motivation is increased, and student understanding is more readily discernible.

5. It serves a variety of purposes through clear transparencies used as a chalkboard; partially prepared transparencies which can be completed with the class; prepared transparencies that illustrate the textbook, current news, graphical presentations, or other supplementary materials; and overlays provide for progressive disclosure and comparison of graphs, concepts, and ideas.

6. It provides for use of commercially prepared transparencies correlated with certain subjects or texts. We believe, however, that the overhead should provide an outlet for an extension of the teacher's personality; and that, in addition to commercially prepared transparencies, the teacher should make transparencies from his own ideas and materials. He will generally make more effective use of those he prepares himself and with which, therefore, he can be at ease in class.

7. It stimulates learning by adding the visual to the auditory appeal. It motivates learning by stimulating interest and curiosity through the presentation.

11.

Use of the Overhead Projector
in Teaching Art and Music

In his famous address before the National Foreign Trade Convention in 1945, American businessman and financier Beardsley Ruml stated, "It takes only a period of about a dozen years to implant a basic culture in the mind of man—the period between the age of two and the age of fourteen."

If this is true, teachers have little time to make children aware of culture in the form of music and art. Of course, the question is always asked, "Is it important to do this?" We can only answer this question by asking another:

Have you ever met a well-rounded and educated person who was not at least appreciative of the cultures? Being a well-rounded individual in our society demands an appreciation and liking for the fine things in life—and the finer things in life include good art and good music.

What can today's school teacher do to foster this appreciation in youngsters who are beset by comic books and insect-named singing groups who sound as melodious as a gang of crickets in chorus. Certainly, it is no longer sufficient to make children listen to music or view art. Students have a way of listening without hearing, and a habit of viewing without seeing. Appreciation of the cultures, educators tell us, can only be attained by understanding them. Therefore, teaching pupils the fundamentals of art and music is more important than hanging up a picture or putting a record on a phonograph. Appreciation without understanding is rarely possible.

To imbue the student with an understanding of art and music in the modern school room, the overhead projector has become as important an aid as the phonograph or the art easel. This is the teaching aid that

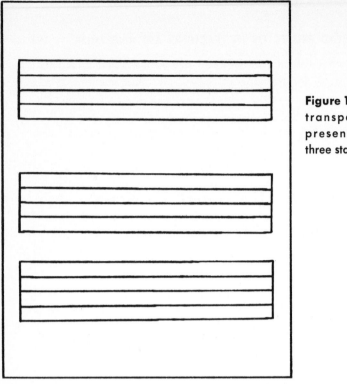

Figure 11.1a. The basic transparency of this presentation contains three staffs.

Figure 11.1b. This is overlay 1, showing leger lines, clefs, and connotations of staff lines and spaces.

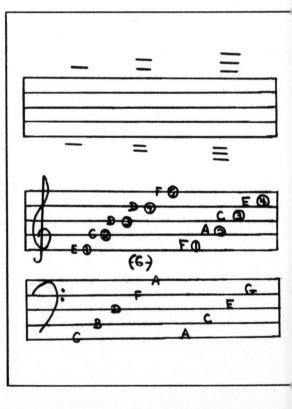

precedes the actual listening or viewing; this is the teaching aid that can be the bulwark for teaching principles and fundamentals. Many schools throughout the country have proved that art and music education are fostered because of projection, as we shall soon see.

There is another aspect to projection which teachers should not overlook. Although of maximum utility in the classroom, there are areas throughout the school where the projector's versatility can come into play. Art teachers, for example, are frequently charged with school displays, bulletin boards, backdrops for school plays, etc. These teachers can make excellent use of the overhead projector's capability as an enlarger for projecting decorative materials, backdrops, bulletin board materials, and school announcements. The projector can be hidden from view, aimed at the bulletin board, backdrop, or what have you, and turned on to project the material.

One interesting music unit entitled, "The ABC's of Music," was originated by teachers at Howard W. Bishop Junior High School in Gainsville, Florida. It could only have been presented via the medium of overhead projector, because it utilizes the extreme versatility of this machine in employing overlay techniques.

Overlays Teach Basic Fundamentals

The unit is a basic one on music fundamentals and was designed primarily for seventh grade level although as you can see, it is equally adaptable to many grade levels and situations. The heart of the unit is a basic transparency and four overlays. All transparencies were made on direct reading image positive films (clear), producing a black image. Color, however, could be used if desired.

The motivating activity is to teach the class and get them to sing the basic "do, re, mi." The theme carried through the entire lesson is that, "When you read, you begin with A-B-C. When you sing, you begin with do-re-mi."

The basic overlay (Figure 11.1a) consists of three staffs. The teaching cycle begins with an explanation of how the staff looks (5 lines, 4 spaces) and why we need it.

Overlay 1 (Figure 11.1b) is then flipped into position. Its purpose is to bring home an understanding of how to extend the staff by means of leger lines above and below it, and the meaning of the bass and treble clefs. Coupled with this is an explanation of the names of lines and spaces for both types of clefs.

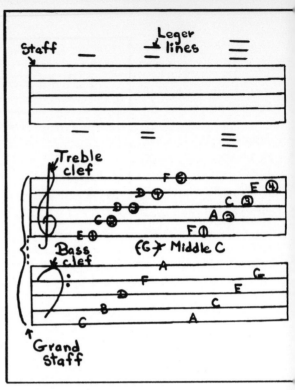

Figure 11.1c. Overlay 2, flipped over the basic transparency and overlay 1, seen in Figures 11.1a and 11.1b, respectively, portray the grand staff.

Figure 11.1d. Overlay 3, placed over the basic transparency, shows notes and rests.

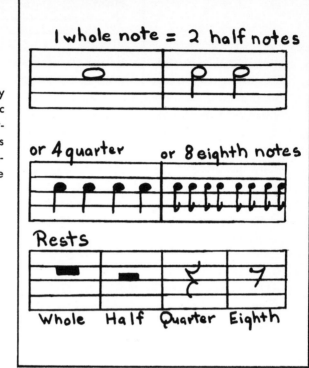

Figure 11.1e. Overlay 4, placed over the basic transparency and overlay 3, seen in Figures 11.1a and 11.1d, respectively, name the notes and the rests.

Overlay 2 (Figure 11.1c) combines everything together under the grand staff. A discussion is held as to its purpose and the way it looks. This overlay also contains nomenclature of subjects previously covered.

For a discussion of notes, overlays 1 and 2 are flipped back out of position and overlays 3 and 4 are used. Overlay 3 (Figure 11.1d) shows the various types of notes and rests. Overlay 4 (Figure 11.1e) names them.

Can you imagine the inadequacy of putting this material on a chalkboard—the inflexibility a chalkboard presents in teaching students these musical fundamentals?

Projector Replaces Chalkboard for Art

"The overhead projector," states an art teacher at the Healy School in Detroit, Michigan, "can be used instead of the chalkboard, in which case it is useful in demonstrating lines, shapes and lettering. By using felt markers, color may be introduced, and it can be easily erased with lighter fluid. Any grease base crayon can also be used, which is very helpful to me in demonstrating the way color can be blended.

"One of the most beneficial techniques for an art class, though, is the flexibility of overlay." She continues, "I use overlay to portray simple sketches to show good and bad designs. Poor details which ruin the balance of a design are drawn on the overlays and then introduced and discussed one at a time. I've also used colored tissue paper, which is transparent enough to show up and which can be overlapped to show the mixing of colors.

"I keep a picture file of reproductions saved over the years from such magazines as *Time* and *Life*," this teacher states. "They include the works of ancient masters, as well as modern artists. These can be reproduced by means of the color lift film and an infrared copying machine and are used in upper grade classes. Pictures of everyday things, special activities and far-away places are also used to motivate, stimulate, and show how design plays such an important part in whatever we do and see."

To illustrate one of her points, the teacher submitted an overlay transparency scheme used to teach the basic principles of design to fourth grade classes. This basic static takes the following form:

1. A checkerboard pattern (Figure 11.2a) is made in black and white using direct reading image positive transparency material. This forms the basic transparency.

2. A checkerboard pattern is then made for overlay 1 (Figure 11.2b). This is done by again reproducing the checkerboard pattern and blacking in every second circle. This portrays a formal design.

3. A second overlay is made by reproducing the checkerboard pattern on a third sheet of transparency film. This time, though, one circle is blackened (Figure 11.2c). When placed over the other two transparencies, this one shows how the eye is attracted to the center of interest.

4. A third overlay is prepared in the same way, but this time two circles are colored different colors to show how one color will stand out over the other and can make the shape appear larger.

Extensive Use of Projection in Music

At Chaminade High School in Dayton, Ohio, the overhead projector is used in every possible musical activity offered by the school. These include glee club, concert band, marching band, music section rehear-

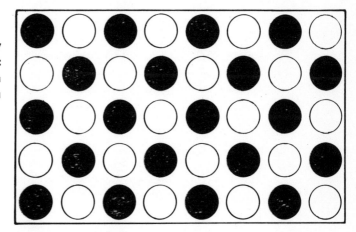

Figure 11.2a. The basic transparency of this presentation on basic art principles is merely a checkerboard pattern.

Figure 11.2b. Overlay 1, flipped over the basic transparency seen in Figure 11.2a, shows a formal design.

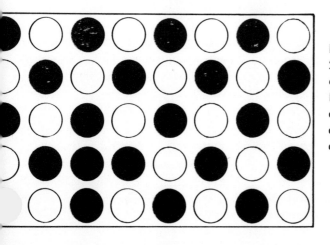

Figure 11.2c. Overlay 2, placed over the preceding ones seen in Figures 11.2a and 11.2b depicts how the eye is attracted to the center of interest.

sals, and in two formal courses titled "Basic Concepts of Music" and "Music Theory and Composition."

Teachers call upon various types of source material for projection including textbook supplements, workbooks, student work, newspapers and magazines, teachers' notes and sketches, and actual musical scores.

For example, to a student not versed in musical instruments a drum might be just a drum. But teachers clip from workbooks and other source material pictures of various types of drums, such as the tympani, snare, and bass. By projection, they are able to show students the differences between them and explain their characteristics and functions. The same technique is used to acquaint students with all types of musical instruments.

Another interesting technique, used especially for the concert band, is a sketch that was part of a teacher's personal file on "Who's Who In a Symphony?" The diagram shows a typical seating arrangement for a symphony orchestra, including the position of a soloist, and portrays the functions of the conductor and concert-master. Students who hitherto were unaware of why or how an orchestra was arranged—most of them probably believed it to be a helter-skelter arrangement—saw in a minute the symmetry, intricacy, and purpose of orchestra seating.

Used in conjunction with this sketch was another portraying what the conductor does, including the importance, position, and purpose of his hand movements. This brought vividly to the music student the importance of keeping an eye on the conductor during the performance of a symphony.

It would be difficult for the teacher to draw these sketches on a chalkboard. Thus, much valuable information for the student could have gone by the wayside if it were not for the speed offered by overhead projection. In just four seconds, a crisp, visually acute transparency was made by placing the transparent film in conjunction with the opaque original and running both through an infrared copying machine. Nothing fancy, to be sure—not even color was used. But the value of the data presented cannot be questioned.

The intricate formations made by a marching band at a football game are wondrous to see, and it leaves many viewers puzzled as to how so many people can get in the exact position without banging trumpets, trombones, clarinets, drums, and heads together. It takes of course, much drill and precision, and now the element of overhead projection has been added to give a valuable assist.

At Chaminade High, before students so much as see the football field for the week's drill preceding a game, the band master assigns each member a code number. He then projects the intricate formation via

Figure 11.3. Intricate band formation for football games can be ironed out before band members assemble on the field. This cuts down the time needed for drill, and permits the band to concentrate on the music.

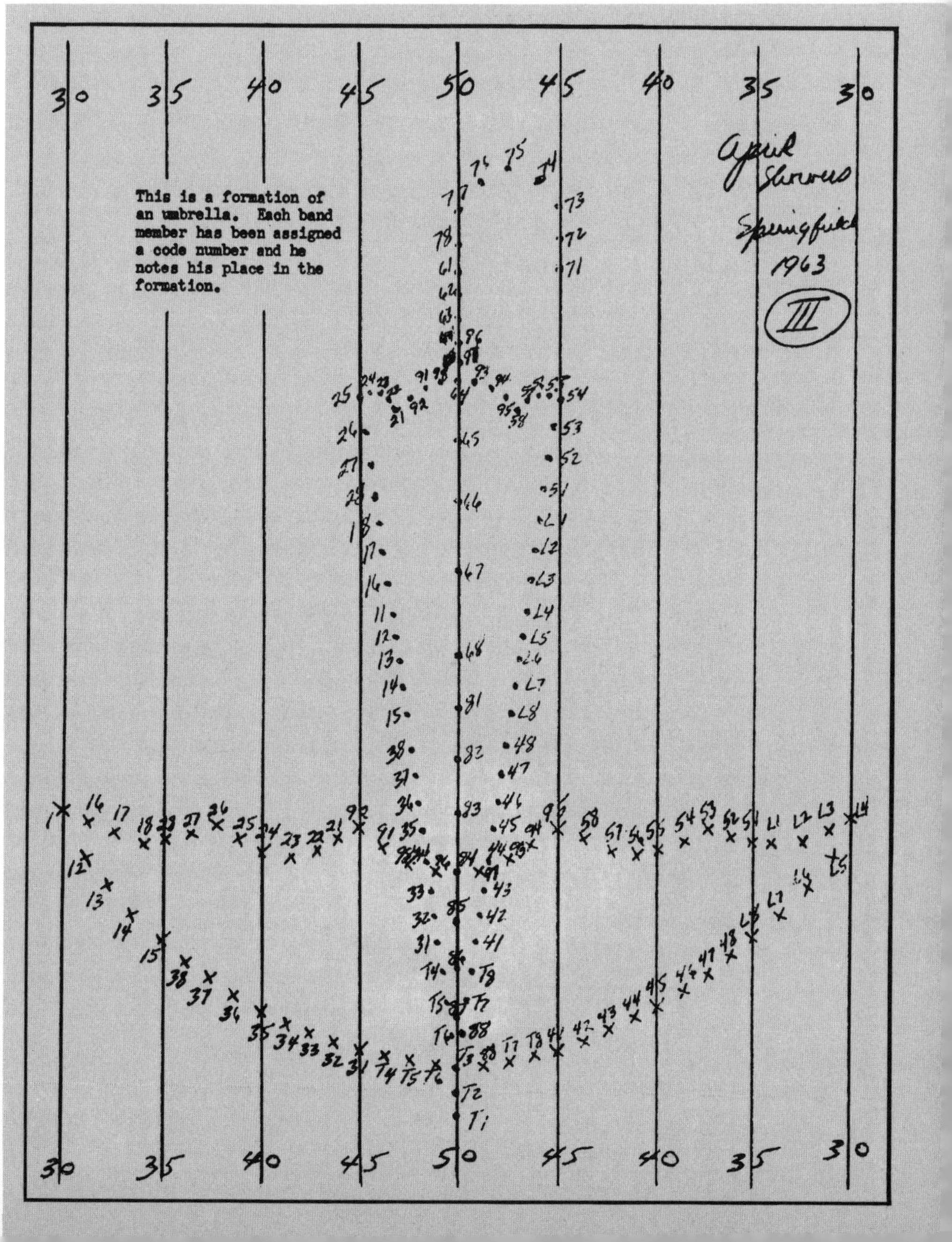

projection, and each member locates his code number and notes his position on the field. When a band member goes onto the field for drill, he has a good idea of where he is supposed to be. This is a decided advantage and, of course, a time-saver thus allowing many more minutes for concentration on music. Figure 11.3 gives you an idea of one such transparency that is used. Naturally, making spirit master copies of this for 75 to 100 band members would be a time-consuming operation for the teacher. With overhead projection, though, he has to make only one reproduction—and that takes but four seconds.

Crafts Education Via Production

In many schools, young children are taught crafts as part of the art program. The overhead projector can be of tremendous advantage here as well.

For example, suppose you wish the children to make a clay model and desire to show them the principles of working with clay. Holding

Figure 11.4. This bead work was done by a second grade student. The teacher attributes his success to the instruction she was able to give him by overhead projection.

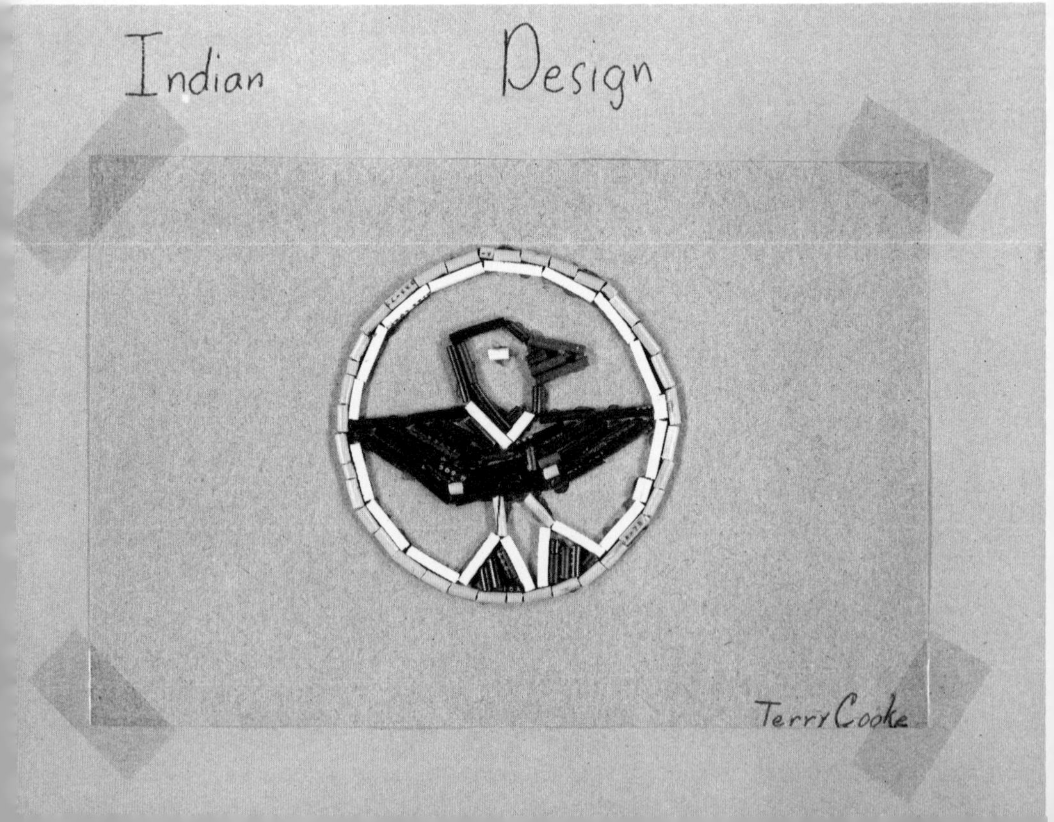

Indian   Design

Terry Cooke

the clay up and trying to manipulate it in mid-air has little advantage. For one thing, it is difficult to handle; for another, only the students close to you can see it clearly.

However, by placing the clay on the projector stage and flashing its outline image onto the screen, you cast this outline and, as you work with the clay, the children, including those in the rear, can see the manipulations and can follow with their own models at their desks.

Figure 11.4 is an example of the end result of this principle. It is bead work done by a lower grade pupil at Lakeside Elementary School in Chattanooga, Tennessee. In doing the design, the student followed the example of the teacher who placed and arranged the beads on the projector stage. The arrangement and manipulations were projected onto the screen.

Projection Helps Students to Draw

At Patti Welder Junior High School in Victoria, Texas, a course in portrait and figure drawing is offered, and the advantages of using overhead projector for this are probably readily apparent to you. The purposes of the course are to learn to get a reasonable facsimile of a living person, to develop in the student the principles of art in portrait drawing, and to develop in them a technique in the use of the medium being used.

Suppose, for example, the teacher is lecturing on the drawing of a head. She takes a sheet of clear transparent film, placing it on the projector, and a grease pencil. As she lectures, she begins to draw, relating the lecture to the drawing. She has the students in their seats following with their own drawing. Such a lecture might proceed as follows:

> The average head is divided into equal parts by a line passing through the corners of the eyes. The upper half reaches to the top of the scalp; the lower to the point of the chin. The tip of the nose is about half the distance from the chin to the line of the eyebrows. A line passing between the lips is half-way between the tip of the nose and the point of the chin. The ears are between the brow line and the nose line. All of these measurements are approximate, as we know that individual differences make up the individual.

The same physical drawing coupled with the spoken word can be used for any segment of a unit on figure drawing. Thus, two essential elements of learning—visual and oral—are always present.

Similar techniques in the use of overhead projection to teach figure drawing are used at Cantrick Junior High School in Monroe, Michigan, and Ravenna High School in Ravenna, Michigan.

We wish here to emphasize one important use of projection in teaching art, as stressed by teachers at Ravenna High, which might otherwise escape us because of its obviousness. Full-color reproduction of major art works or, for that matter, most full-color pictures if composed on suitable stock, can be made into full color transparencies by use of the color lift process (see Chapter 2). This is the act of taking a full color original, placing it into contact with a special color lift transparency film, and running both through the infrared copying machine. In seconds, the full color of the original is transferred to the film and is ready for projection—in full color. As emphasized before in this book, the only disadvantage to the process is that the original is destroyed since the color is actually lifted right off it.

Uses in Music Summarized

The music department at Mater Dei High School in Santa Ana, California, uses overhead projection in several ways, a few of which

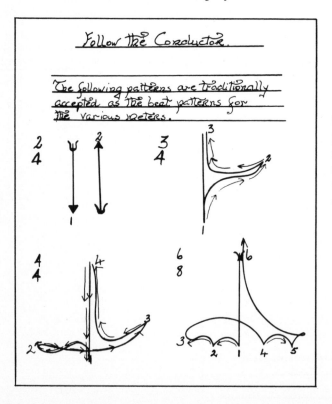

Figure 11.5. This transparency is used to help students understand the traditional hand patterns used by symphony conductors.

Figure 11.6. A transparency such as this can show students how two great maestros, Stokowski and Toscanini, arranged their orchestra members for various musical effects. The lesson can be further heightened by presenting compositions of both via the phonograph and pointing out to students these effects.

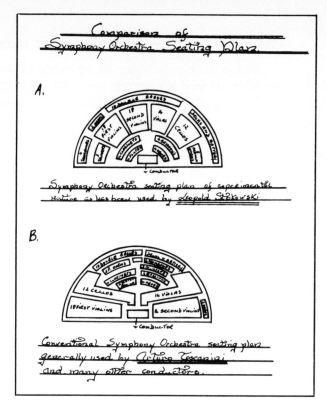

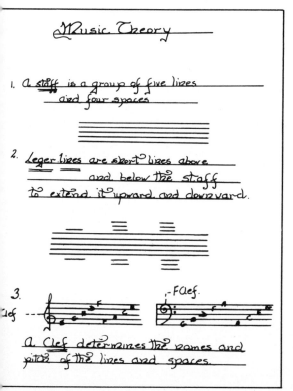

Figure 11.7. As simple as it appears, this transparency could be invaluable in getting across musical theory.

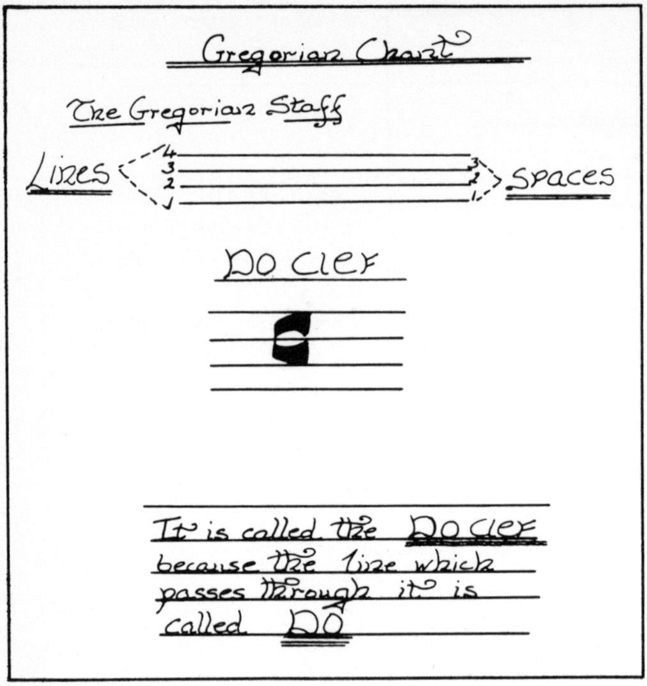

Figure 11.8. When pupils can see as well as hear something, it makes a greater imprint on their minds than if they simply hear words from a teacher.

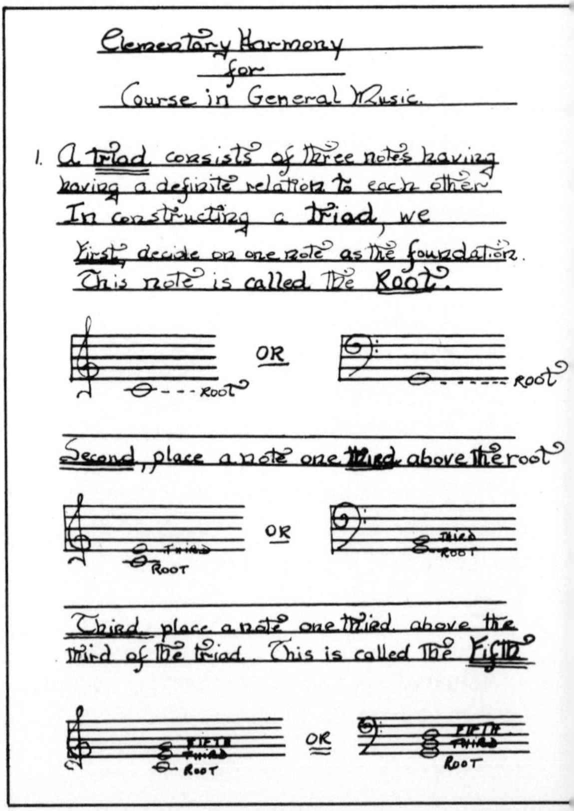

Figure 11.9. This transparency, simple in make-up, shows the steps in constructing a triad.

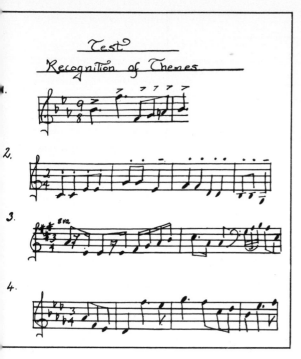

Figure 11.10. Music can be best appreciated by listening to it and seeing it. The two used together can imbue students with an appreciation for this fine culture.

have been mentioned previously. However, we shall list them to sum up these methods for you:

1. To teach fundamentals of conducting patterns (Figure 11.5).

2. To show and compare two different seating arrangements for a symphony orchestra (Figure 11.6).

3. To present the instruments of the orchestra to a general music class.

4. To teach the fundamentals of music theory, such as staff, leger lines, clefs, and so forth (Figure 11.7).

5. To introduce the Gregorian Chant (Figure 11.8).

6. To teach harmony. In building triads, for example, each step can be clearly seen by means of projection (Figure 11.9).

7. To acquaint students with theme recognition. While the students listen to the theme being played on the phonograph, they may follow the theme as it is written because it is being projected (Figure 11.10).

Teaching Art Perspective

A marvelous use of the overlay technique is employed by an art teacher at Ezra C. Fitch and Chauncey Newhall Schools in Waltham,

Massachusetts. The purpose of the lesson is to study perspective, and particularly the principles of three vanishing points in achieving the end result which, in this case, is a house. All transparencies were made on clear direct reading image positive film, and color was introduced to emphasize solid formations and add "life" to the presentation.

Figure 11.11a is the basic transparency mounted in a frame. Overlay 1 (Figure 11.11b) introduces horizontal lines to impress the first step in the formation.

Overlay 2 (Figure 11.11c) is the first introduction of color. The solid "wall" is colored in with blue grease pencil. Overlay 3 (Figure 11.11d introduces additional perspective elements, and Overlay 4 (Figure 11.11e), with additional color for the peak, roof and chimney, completes the project.

Any student witnessing how this drawing takes form from simple lines is quick to grasp the simplicity of it and the importance of perspective to drawing. This type of presentation is, of course, not possible with any other but overhead projection techniques.

An arts and crafts teacher at Valley Regional High School in Deep River, Connecticut, states, "As an art teacher, I make transparencies of paintings to develop a better understanding for the student and assist

Figure 11.11a. This is the basic transparency used in teaching art perspective.

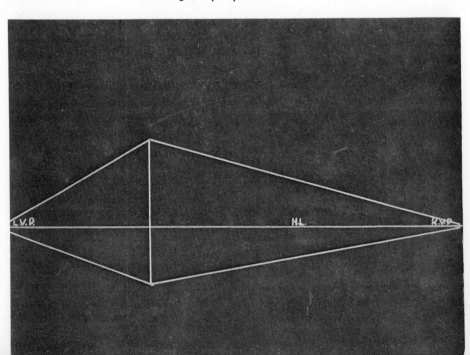

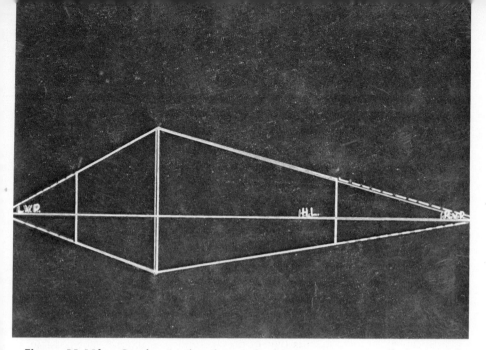

Figure 11.11b. Overlay 1, placed over the basic transparency seen in Figure 11.11a, shows a breakup of lines in the basic transparency—the first step in this construction.

Figure 11.11c. The formation begins to take shape with the introduction of overlay 2, which portrays the first solid configuration.

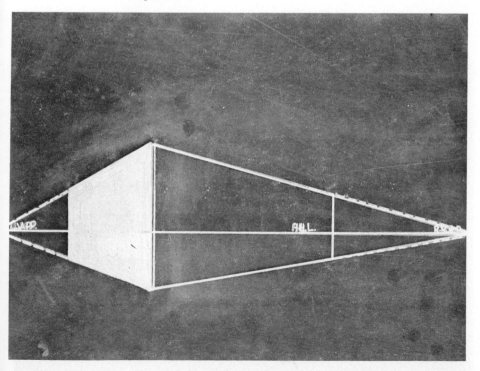

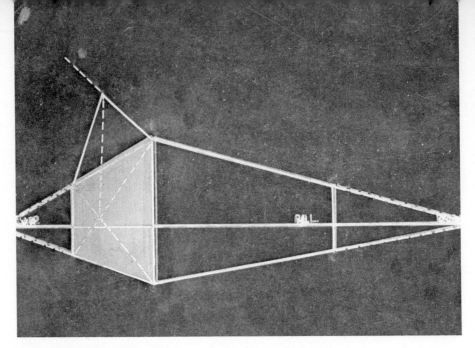

Figure 11.11d. Overlay 3 projects the lines in preparation for the final formation.

Figure 11.11e. Overlay 4, showing the final formation, also emphasizes the perspective theme.

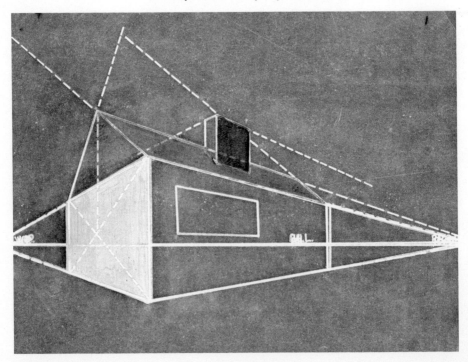

him in art appreciation. I also use transparencies while teaching perspective, lettering, or for that matter, all types of art principles. Transparencies are most helpful, as well, in demonstrating shading while sketching, since one has black against white, as it should be, instead of the reverse offered by a chalkboard."

To emphasize the point to students that a mass or solid is confined by lines, this teacher uses the transparencies seen in Figures 11.12a and 11.12b. Figure 11.12a is a solid mass, as you can see.

"But, children, look at the magic. This solid mass is actually composed of and confined inside lines," and Figure 11.12b—the overlay—is flipped into position.

Figure 11.12a. To students, this transparency when projected looks like a solid formation.

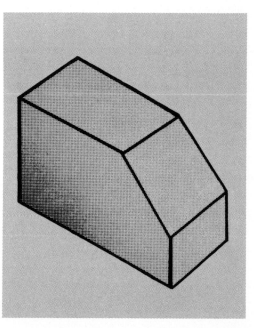

Figure 11.12b. When the overlay is placed over the basic transparency of Figure 11.12a, a student quickly sees that a mass takes line form.

Art Lesson Plan for Your Use

The author was quite fortunate in being offered a complete art lesson plan for use in this book by officials at Saint Mary's Central High School in Bismarck, North Dakota. I say "fortunate," because it gives us an opportunity to discuss with you how a lesson can progress and develop. For this reason, we are taking the liberty of presenting the plan in its entirety.

The general teaching aim of the lesson is to help students obtain a feeling of nearness and farness in their drawings. The specific teaching aim is to teach students the simple basic rules of perspective. The aim of the students is to learn these simple rules.

Materials utilized during the lesson are the overhead projector, transparent material, carbon pencil, and a ruler. The teacher activity is as follows:

Introduction: I am sure you have all seen a road stretched across the prairies. If you were traveling on this road, you could see that the road is somewhat larger than the width of two cars placed side-by-side. Yet, the farther away the road goes, the narrower it becomes until, finally, it seems no wider than a pinpoint. The road vanishes on the horizon line—the line that separates the sky from the earth. This line is also level with the eye. The point at which the road seems to disappear is called the vanishing point. The area within a picture is called a picture plain.

The body of the lesson proceeds as follows:

Now that we have established a horizon line at our eye level on a picture plain, we will need a vanishing point.

(At this point, the teacher demonstrates on the projector with carbon pencil and clear transparency film the picture frame, horizon line, and vanishing point.)

All lines which do not run parallel with our picture frame lines converge to the vanishing point. Remember that only diagonal lines run to the vanishing point.

(The teacher demonstrates this point by drawing a simple box in perspective. It is pointed out that the top of objects above eye level (or the horizon line) cannot be seen; that objects established below eye level show the top of their form. A series of different drawings are drawn showing objects below and above the horizon line.)

At this point, a student activity is introduced. The students are assigned to draw a one-point perspective street scene. The buildings are developed from the simple box form. During the course of the period, incorrect observations on the part of the students can be corrected for the benefit of all by making a transparency from their work. It is easily done by running work and transparency film through the infrared copying machine, which takes but four seconds. This is, of course, a great time saver. When the students are ready for small detailed work, such as windows in the buildings, the teacher once more demonstrates on the overhead projector the division of a surface in perspective.

The teacher's activity to this end proceeds as follows:

> First divide the near side into the number of parts you wish. Carry these lines to the vanishing point. Next draw a diagonal line from one corner of the surface rectangle to the other. Where the lines cross, draw horizontal or vertical lines. This will divide your surface correctly and proportionately.

This concludes the lesson, but the teacher using it points out that there are other uses for projection in perspective lessons. She states that "circles in perspective are difficult to demonstrate on the chalkboard. The overhead projector is excellent in demonstrating this project. Other projects that could be carried out are the more than one vanishing point perspective."

Similar methods of teaching perspective are used by teachers in many other schools, including Northeast Intermediate School in Midland, Michigan, and Pasadena High School in Pasadena, Texas.

Overlay Helps in Teaching
Notes, Time, and Rests

A particularly attractive overlay arrangement, utilizing color for emphasis, is used by music teachers at Memorial Elementary School in Garden City, Michigan, to teach younger students notes, time, and rests. The display is seen in Figure 11.13. Note the basic transparency. Numbers beneath the four others are the overlays which are introduced in this order and progressively. Once an overlay is introduced, it is kept in position over the preceding transparencies.

As you can see, the basic transparency shows the whole note, the count it receives, and the rest symbol. This is prepared as a black image on a sheet of clear direct image reading positive film.

Overlay 1 shows the transformation of the whole note to a half note.

Again, its count and rest symbol are revealed. The staff of the half note and the rest are colored in red, as is the explanation "2 counts." Note also that there are only four staffs to transform four of the whole notes into half notes. One whole note is kept whole so the pupil can have both in view at the same time. This basic pattern is followed throughout the remainder of the presentation.

Overlay 2 shows the transformation of half notes into quarter notes, their rest, and count. The overlay is colored blue.

Overlay 3 shows eighth notes and is colored in green, and *Overlay 4* shows sixteenth notes and is colored in violet. Both portray, as well, the rest symbol and count.

When the arrangement is put together, the student is able to see the transformation of musical notes from whole to sixteenth and their rest

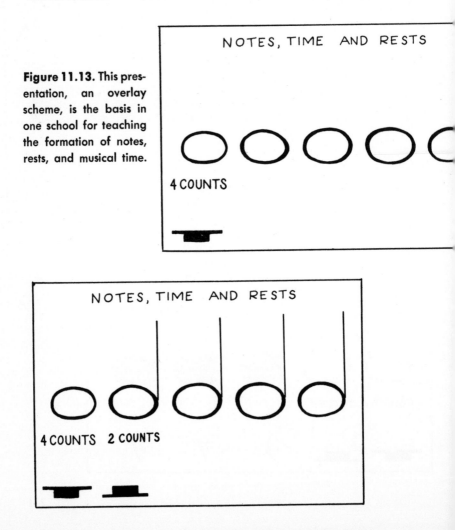

Figure 11.13. This presentation, an overlay scheme, is the basis in one school for teaching the formation of notes, rests, and musical time.

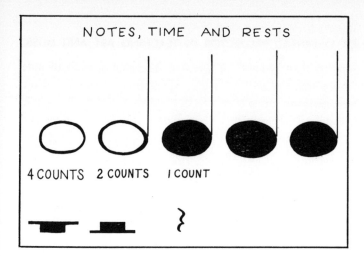

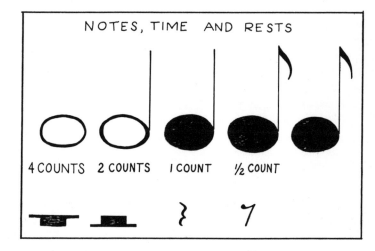

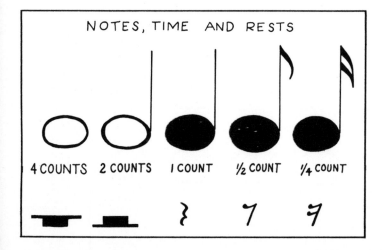

symbols. Naturally, when viewed in this manner the essentials of note count are best typified.

More Than One Use

An overlay transparency, as we have stressed many times in this book, can serve more than one purpose. Look, for example, at Figures

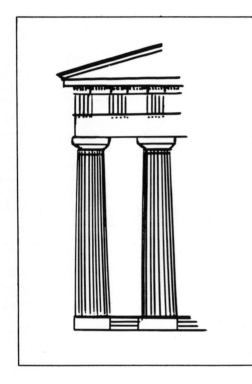

Figure 11.14a. This transparency is used in a lecture.

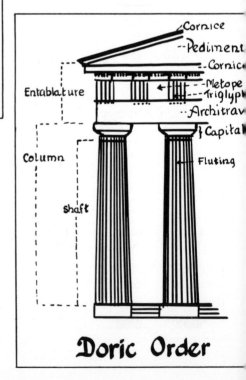

11.14a and 11.14b, which are employed in a course in art history at Dominican College of San Rafael in San Rafael, California.

The first overlay (Figure 11.14a), flipped over a basic transparency of a Greek Temple of the Doric Order, names the parts of the temple. It is used for the lecture.

The second overlay (Figure 11.14b) is composed of the same Greek

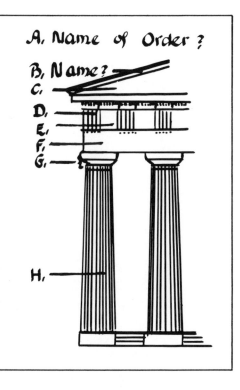

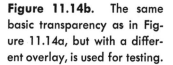

Figure 11.14b. The same basic transparency as in Figure 11.14a, but with a different overlay, is used for testing.

Temple as the basic overlay. Now, however, the overlay asks the students to name some of the parts. It is used for examination.

These, then, are some of the many ways in which overhead projection can be used for the benefit of a class in teaching students the cultures of art and music. As with the other subjects in this book, it is admitted quite frankly that there might be many other employments for which projection can be utilized, some of which only you may be able to think of. Since this book, as stated before, has the dual purpose of introducing you to the possibilities of projection utilization and stressing that imagination is a requisite for employment, we feel we have accomplished our purposes in this chapter concerned with overhead projection and its use in art and musical education.

12.

Use of the Overhead Projector
in Teaching Other Subjects

To this point, we have dealt in this book with the use of overhead projection in teaching subjects that are most common to all school curriculums. The author is certain that you can understand the impracticality of dealing with all subjects offered on a grade, secondary, and college levels. Not only would it make for a voluminous work, but it would be most repetitious, leading to boredom on the part of the reader. As we have continually stressed throughout, what applies to one subject regarding projection, usually applies to all. The teacher of any subject, then, can utilize the basics of projection portrayed throughout this book to his own subject.

To culminate our discussion, however, we wish in this chapter to touch on overhead projection utilization in other subject areas—specifically, physical education and home economics. Again, let us stress that the basic techniques of projection used in these areas can well apply to yours. The only thing that will change is, of course, the nature of the transparencies themselves.

Of Value in Physical Education

The following are comments regarding overhead projection made by members of the athletic staff at Patti Welder Junior High School in Victoria, Texas:

> I believe that the overhead projector is very beneficial when actual court instruction is not possible. The projector is an excellent teaching aid in that I can reconstruct actual tennis court situations. Tennis court drawings are projected with emphasis on court positioning, boundary lines, the volley, score-keeping, footwork,

the service, and strategy. The projector is also used as a testing aid by combining aforementioned situations. I feel that the projector has definitely benefited the tennis program, as well as the whole athletic program at Patti Welder Junior High.

We, the coaching staff, feel that the overhead projector is one of the most valuable aids for our football team. Most of the information has heretofore been presented on the chalkboard, but projection now saves us time and, in our football season, this is an important factor. We must save time and make use of every minute. Transparencies can be saved for future reference, especially during

Figure 12.1. A chart such as this flashed on a screen via projection outlines in quick order the points the teacher is establishing.

bad weather when it is not possible to work outdoors. As the season progresses we add to our offense and defense. We present different drills by means of transparencies. In short, we highly recommend this important aid for presentation of football material.

Several excellent examples of the use to which overhead projection can be put in a physical education and health program were submitted by Medill Bair High School in Fairless Hills, Pennsylvania. Figure 12.1, for example, is a transparency used in the classroom as part of a health personality unit. The teacher found this a much better way to present instructional material than by a straightforward lecture or by making a list or two on a chalkboard.

Figures 12.2 and 12.3 portray instructional material in life-saving functions. Figure 12.2, to show the progressive steps in mouth-to-mouth resuscitation, employs the revelation technique. In use, each of the four blocks has a cardboard square over it, thus blocking out the image from the screen. As the teacher discusses a step, a cardboard block is

Figure 12.2. This transparency, which uses revelation, is excellent in teaching mouth-to-mouth resuscitation.

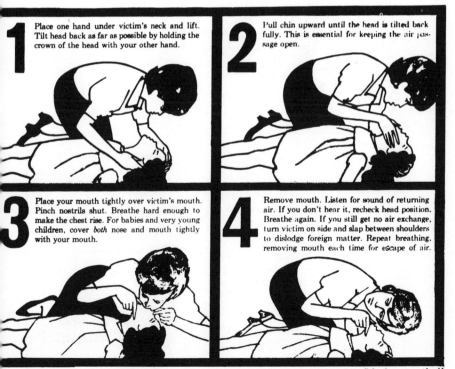

1. Place one hand under victim's neck and lift. Tilt head back as far as possible by holding the crown of the head with your other hand.

2. Pull chin upward until the head is tilted back fully. This is essential for keeping the air passage open.

3. Place your mouth tightly over victim's mouth. Pinch nostrils shut. Breathe hard enough to make the chest rise. For babies and very young children, cover *both* nose and mouth tightly with your mouth.

4. Remove mouth. Listen for sound of returning air. If you don't hear it, recheck head position. Breathe again. If you still get no air exchange, turn victim on side and slap between shoulders to dislodge foreign matter. Repeat breathing, removing mouth each time for escape of air.

Step-by-step progression in the teaching of mouth-to-mouth resuscitation (block-out method)

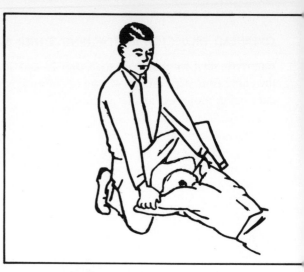

Figure 12.3. The progressive steps in artificial respiration, when used in overlay, give one the impact of a motion picture.

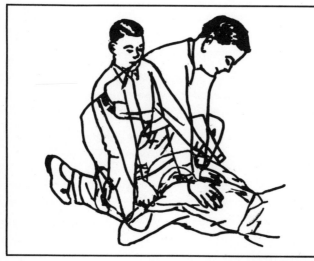

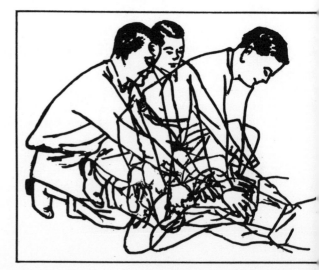

218

removed—first from step 1, then step 2, and so forth. This is done so the entire four steps are not shown at one time, thus distracting from the data being presented at the moment.

Figure 12.3 utilizes the overlay technique and shows the progression of artificial respiration. The first of the series shows the arm-lift, while the remainder shows the back pressure. With one overlay placed on top of another, the students get the impression of progression in artificial respiration, much the same as if they were watching a motion picture on the subject.

All examples, by the way, were made from originals that were in a teacher's file. Their actual reproduction into transparency form was simple enough. The teacher simply placed the original in contact with a sheet of direct reading image positive film and ran the two through an infrared copying machine. The transparency was ready in just four seconds.

Projection Proves an Effective "Coach"

There is perhaps no better use to which overhead projection can be put in the area of physical education than in instructing team members. The utilization of projection for this is perhaps no better exemplified than in football. We feel the uses of projection in this area were best summed up by the football coaching staff at West Jefferson High School in Harvey, Louisiana.

Of the many practical uses of the overhead projector that we have found in physical education, its value in the explanation of football plays is perhaps the greatest. There are many reasons for this observation. Principally, however, are the following:

1. With a basic formation drawn on the transparency, and with grease pencils, we can demonstrate the right and wrong method at the same time.

2. On option plays, we can point out several methods of development without having to erase or change the pattern as would be necessary on a chalkboard.

3. In facing the players while explaining, we can better read the depth of their understanding of the subject.

One of the most vital aspects of coaching is the presentation of game tactics in the form of plays designed and presented to the players by the coach. These diagrams are drawn in detail and explained accordingly. It is essential that these plays are learned as they are presented. Overhead projection is used to present them to the team. There is, of course, no problem in showing them to large groups in a gym, since the image is magnified. The plays are explained and elaborated on by the coach as he presents them. They can be prepared prior to a meeting or can be drawn right on the projector stage as the coach shows development of a play and various options. There is never any problem in depicting detailed patterns or indicating movements. This information is then filed and used by the coaching staff again and again, thus saving a great deal of time in mimeographing study guides. Naturally, the transparencies are made available to any individual player who requests them at any time so that he can review his assignment for any play.

As a coach, you should keep in mind that color can be used on transparency material. For example, suppose you wish to portray a particular play for a team. You can use different colored grease pencils or felt markers to depict the various functionaries in development of the play. For example, red can be used to show the movement of the ball, blue to show the position of the players, green to show the movement of the players, and black to show the opposing team.

Projection Applied to Home Economics

The subject of home economics is one that readily applies itself to overhead projection. "While we recognize that the overhead projector is an invaluable teaching tool in any field," claims a home economics teacher at Bakersfield High School in Bakersfield, California,

> we feel it is a dynamic addition to home economics classes. We do not have textbooks for all units because of these reasons:
>
> Ours is an ever-changing field. New discoveries in the biological and physical sciences, plus new theories and the results of improved research in the behavorial sciences mean that for us textbooks ever lag behind. Consequently, we rely heavily on monthly publications, as well as on materials that we previously had to mimeograph. In essence we often must "write" our own texts as we progress.
>
> Home economics is a flexible subject matter area where the curriculum must be tailor-made to fit local school conditions. Thus, textbooks published for nationwide consumption are frequently not satisfactory for a particular school condition. At Bakersfield High, we are unique and fortunate that our home economics classes are taught at three achievement levels. Unfortunately, though, textbooks are not written at three levels in our field.

There is a further reason why overhead projectors are highly desirable in home economics classes. Ours is a broad field. We actually have little subject matter of our own. Instead we "borrow" from many other disciplines topics that we apply to the home and family. To be adequately prepared for our classrooms takes a great deal of time. And the countless hours we would have to spend in preparing our own visual aids is drastically cut with an overhead.

To illustrate these broad points, here is a list of materials that can be prepared in transparency form for use in home economics classes. The list was established by home economics teachers at Flagstaff High School in Flagstaff, Arizona:

A. Clothing
  1. Color units
    a. Start with primary colors, add secondary and intermediate overlays.
    b. Start with one primary color, use overlays of white and black to show value changes.
    c. Start with one color, use overlays of complementary colors to show intensity changes.
  2. Effect of lines, colors, fabric designs on apparent figure size
    a. Have two figures and add overlays to show what happens with various lines, colors, and fabric designs.
  3. Historical influence in design
    a. Transparencies of historical costumes to point out the basic designs that have been used through the years.
    b. Transparencies of modern dress that show definite historical influences.

B. Home Management
  1. House Plans
    a. Transparencies of different floor plans for various studies
      1) Traffic patterns
      2) Living areas
      3) Furniture placement
      4) Room sizes
    b. Charts showing family life cycle, up-to-date income charts, budget percentages, etc.
    c. Color transparencies of furnishings to put into transparency of plain room; effect of warm and cool colors, light and dark colors.
  2. Baby and mother care unit
    a. Transparencies showing development of fetus made according to scale.

    b. Various other charts that would make the teaching of
       this unit easier, as this material is not readily available.
 3. Home nursing unit
    a. Use of transparencies to demonstrate steps in home nursing
       instruction techniques before physical demonstrations are
       actually attempted.

Examples Cited

Figures 12.4 through 12.8b portray how some of the aforementioned
material, which is rarely presented in a textbook, can be used in home
economics classes.

Figure 12.4, as you can see, is a transparency that brings vividly into
focus various cuts of meat. The points "What to Look For When Buy-

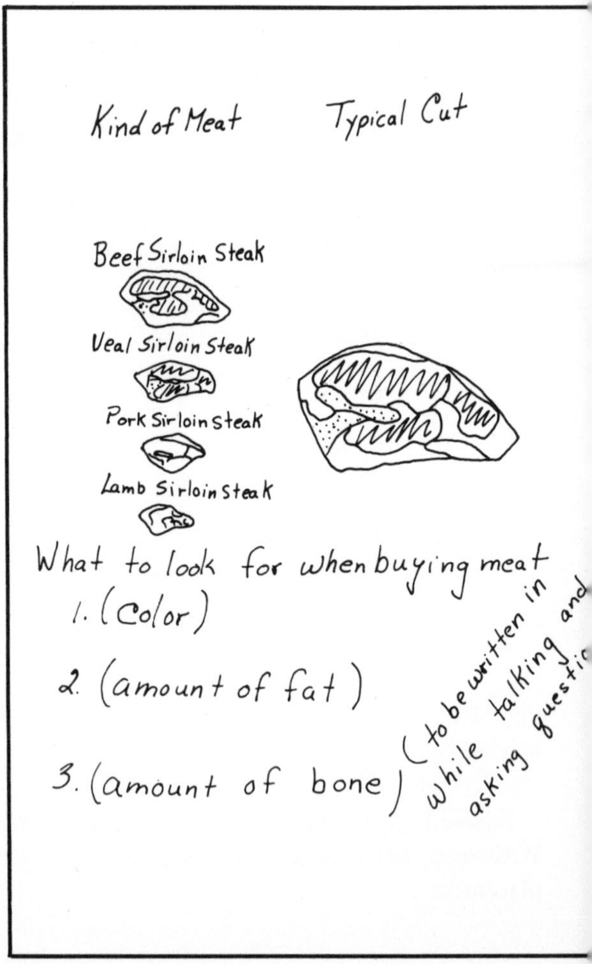

Figure 12.4. A transparency that shows cuts of meat and what to look for when buying meat is helpful to future homemakers.

Kind of Meat   Typical Cut

Beef Sirloin Steak

Veal Sirloin Steak

Pork Sirloin Steak

Lamb Sirloin Steak

What to look for when buying meat
1. (Color)
2. (amount of fat)
3. (amount of bone)

(to be written in while talking and asking questio

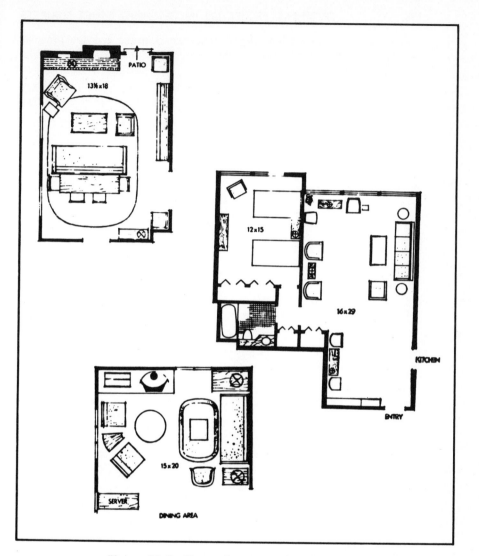

Figure 12.5. Since a home can't be brought into the classroom, overhead projection transparencies showing floor plans and furniture arrangements are the next best thing.

ing Meat" are written on the transparency with grease pencil by the teacher as the lecture progresses. This example was submitted by teachers at Easton Junior High School in Easton, Pennsylvania.

Figure 12.5, submitted by teachers at Central High School in Madison, Wisconsin, portrays to students what is involved in effective furniture placement.

Figures 12.6 through 12.8b have been submitted by Southwest Junior High School in Little Rock, Arkansas. They depict excellent utilization of transparencies in three different home economics areas.

Figures 12.6a through 12.6g are overlays that show the proper development of a dinner place setting. The diagrams are simple and the

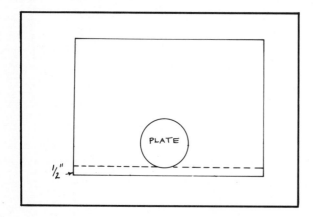

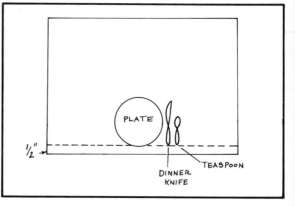

Figure 12.6a-12.6g. These are the progressive parts of an overlay scheme to show home economic students how to arrange a dinner place setting properly.

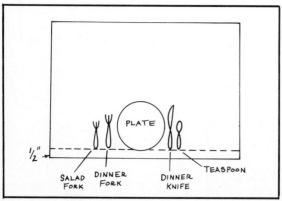

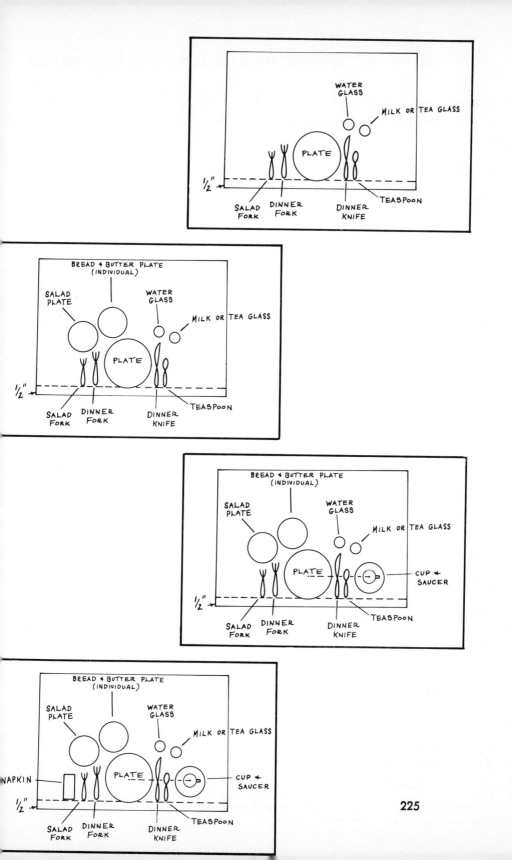

225

To Shorten a Pattern

Front Bodice

Sleeve

Skirt Front

- How To Alter Your Pattern -
- To Lengthen -
To Shorten a Pattern

Front Bodice

Skirt Front

Sleeve

Figures 12.7a-12.7b. These two transparencies can either be used individually or in overlay fashion.

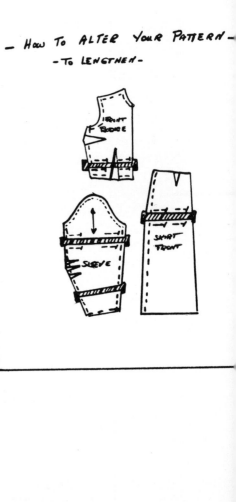

- How To Alter Your Pattern -
- To Lengthen -

Front Bodice

Sleeve

Skirt Front

only critical factor was to make sure each overlay was in proper registration with the preceding one. In other words, to make sure that each of the utensils shown as the place setting developed for the students was in proper relation to the ones shown previously. (For further explanation of registration, see Chapter 2.)

Figures 12.7a and 12.7b also utilize the overlay technique. Figure 12.7a shows how to shorten a pattern, while Figure 12.7b when placed over Figure 12.7a shows how to lengthen a pattern.

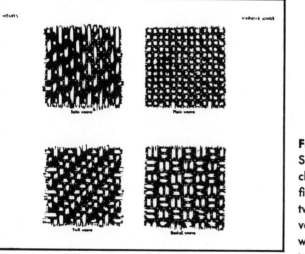

Figures 12.8a - 12.8b. Simply reproduced on a clear sheet of positive film and in black, these two transparencies reveal in a few minutes what might otherwise take an hour to discuss.

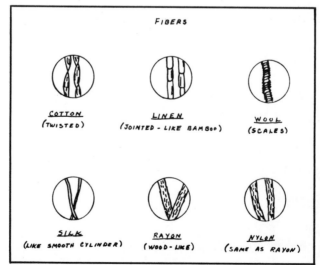

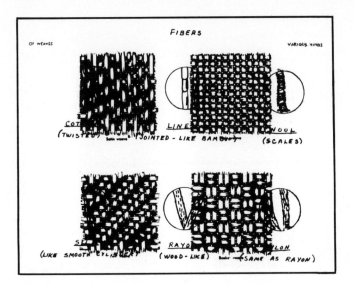

Figures 12.8a and 12.8b portray the physical characteristics of fibers and the four basic weaves. They can be used separately or together in overlay fashion.

Appendix

There are several makes and models of overhead projectors being sold. In addition, many manufacturing firms produce transparent materials and other equipment needed to incorporate an overhead projection capability into a school.

This appendix is devoted to a listing of companies who manufacture and produce equipment and materials for overhead projection. It is offered with the expectation that the teacher will make use of it in securing information regarding these products. Each of the manufacturers mentioned has gone on record as being more than willing to correspond with teachers concerning their projection needs. All have available descriptive literature concerning their products.

Overhead Projectors

1. American Optical Company
   Instrument Division
   Buffalo 15, New York

2. Bausch & Lomb, Inc.
   Instrument Sales Division
   635 St. Paul Street
   Rochester 2, New York

3. Charles Beseler Company
   219 South 18th Street
   East Orange, New Jersey

4. Buhl Optical Company
   1009 Beech Avenue
   Pittsburgh 33, Pennsylvania

5. Keystone View Company
   Meadville, Pennsylvania

6. Laboratory Furniture Co., Inc.
   Old Country Road
   PO Box 590
   Mineola, New York

7. E. Leitz, Inc.
   468 Park Avenue South
   New York 16, New York

8. Minnesota Mining and
      Manufacturing Company
   2501 Hudson Road
   St. Paul, Minnesota

9. Ozalid Division
   General Aniline and Film
      Corporation
   Johnson City, New York

10. Projection Optics Company, Inc.
    271 Eleventh Avenue
    East Orange, New Jersey

11. Technifax Corporation
    Holyoke, Massachusetts

12. Victorlite Industries, Inc.
    4117 West Jefferson Boulevard
    Los Angeles 16, California

Copying Machines, Thermo-Fax Process (Dry)

Minnesota Mining and Manufacturing Company
2501 Hudson Road
St. Paul, Minnesota

Copying Machines, Transferon-Reflex Process (Wet)

1. American Photocopy
   Equipment Company
   2100 West Dempster Street
   Evanston, Illinois

2. Ampto, Inc.
   Anken Chemical and Film
   Corporation
   Hicks Avenue
   Newton, New Jersey

3. Charles Beseler Company
   219 South 18th Street
   East Orange, New Jersey

4. Charles Bruning Company
   1800 West Central
   Mt. Prospect, Illinois

5. Copease Corporation
   20 Fremont Street
   San Francisco, California

6. Copy-Craft, Inc.
   105 Chambers Street
   New York 7, New York

7. Cormac Photocopy Corporation
   80 Fifth Avenue
   New York 11, New York

8. A. B. Dick Company
   5700 West Touhy Avenue
   Chicago 31, Illinois

9. Eastman Kodak Company
   Rochester, New York

10. General Photo Products
    Company
    Box 23
    Chatham, New Jersey

11. Ideax Corporation
    150 Fifth Avenue
    New York, New York

12. F. G. Ludwig, Inc.
    Coulter Street
    Old Saybrook, Connecticut

13. Keuffel and Esser Company
    Adams and Third Streets
    Hoboken, New Jersey

14. Nord Photocopy Corporation
    300 Denton Avenue
    New Hyde Park, Long Island,
    New York

15. Peerless Photo Products
    Route 25A
    Shoreham, Long Island,
    New York

16. Photorapid Corporation
    126 Fifth Avenue
    New York 1, New York

17. Frederick Post Company
    3650 North Avondale Avenue
    Chicago 18, Illinois

18. Royal McBee Corporation
    1700 Wisconsin Avenue, NW
    Washington, D. C.

19. Viewfex, Inc.
    Holbrook, Long Island, New
    York

20. Webster Brothers Laboratory
    2049 West Chase Avenue
    Chicago 45, Illinois

Screens

1. Da-Lite Screen Company, Inc.
   Warsaw, Indiana

2. Hunter-Douglas Division

Bridgeport Brass Company
30 Grand Street
Bridgeport 2, Connecticut

3. Radiant Manufacturing
   Company

8220 North Austin Avenue
Morton Grove, Illinois

Ready-Made Transparencies

1. Admaster Prints, Inc.
   425 Park Avenue South
   New York 16, New York

2. Robert J. Brady Company
   3227 M Street, NW
   Washington 7, D.C.

3. State University of Iowa
   Bureau of Audiovisual
     Instruction
   Extension Division
   Iowa City, Iowa

4. McGraw-Hill Book Company,
   Inc.

330 West 42nd Street
New York 36, New York

5. DCA Educational Products, Inc.
   4865 Stenton Avenue
   Philadelphia, Pennsylvania

6. RCA Educational Services
   Camden 8, New Jersey

7. Technifax Corporation
   Holyoke, Massachusetts

8. Tweedy Transparencies
   321 Central Avenue
   Newark 3, New Jersey

Materials and Services for Making
Your Own Transparencies

1. Admaster Prints, Inc.
   425 Park Avenue South
   New York 16, New York

2. Charles Beseler Company
   219 South 18th Street
   East Orange, New Jersey

3. Robert J. Brady Company
   3227 M Street, NW
   Washington 7, D.C.

4. Keystone View Company
   Meadville, Pennsylvania

5. Keuffel and Esser Company

Audiovisual Division
Hoboken, New Jersey

6. Minnesota Mining and
     Manufacturing Company
   2501 Hudson Road
   St. Paul, Minnesota

7. Ozalid Division
   General Aniline and Film
     Corporation
   Johnson City, New York

8. Technifax Corporation
   Holyoke, Massachusetts

Publisher's Compatible Materials List

Here is a listing of textbooks, workbooks, or Atlases that are considered compatible with Overhead Projection. By compatible with Overhead Projection, it is meant that:

1. The illustrations within certain workbooks and Atlases are of sufficient size (letter and diagram), as they exist.

2. Where the original drawing within the text or workbook is not large enough, the publisher is providing blown-up illustrations in a separate supplement or teacher's manual.

3. These publishers are working with the 3M Company in an effort to meet the needs of teachers. They have stated that the material is copyrighted, but also have said that it is quite ethical and acceptable from their standpoint for teachers to prepare an Overhead Transparency for classroom demonstration purposes.

All inquiries relative to the availability and cost of these materials should be directed to the publisher.

JOHN WILEY & SONS, INC.
440 Park Ave. South
New York 16, N. Y.

Book	Subject Area	Grade Level
Essentials of Healthier Living	Health & Physical Education	S, C
Atlas of Drawings for Chordate Anatomy	Biological Sciences	C

PROFESSIONAL PRODUCTIONS, INC., TAMA Division
608 Second Ave. South
Minneapolis, Minnesota

My Health	Health & Physical Education	K
Physical Fitness and Me	Health & Physical Education	E

NOBLE & NOBLE PUBLISHER, INC.
67 Irving Place
New York 3, New York

Better Handwriting for Everyone (Series)	Handwriting	E
Catholic School Handwriting Series	Handwriting	E

E. C. SEALE & CO.
Indianapolis 20, Indiana

I Learn to Write (Series)	Handwriting	E

CHARLES E. MERRILL BOOKS,
    INC.
1300 Alum Creek Drive
Columbus 16, Ohio

Book	Subject Area	Grade Level
Algebra One: A Modern Course	Mathematics	S
Algebra Two: A Modern Course	Mathematics	S
Geometry: A Unified Course	Mathematics	S
Outline Maps	Social Science	E, S

BURGESS PUBLISHING CO.
426 S. Sixth Street
Minneapolis, Minnesota

Let's Alter Your Pattern (1959)	Home Economics	C
It's So, Sew Easy (1962)	Home Economics	C
Interior Design (4th Ed. 1961)	Home Economics	C
Flat Pattern Methods (1961)	Home Economics	C
Workbook for Introductory Anthropology (1962)	Social Sciences	C
Invertebrate Zoology (Lab Workbook—2nd Ed. 1962)	Biological Sciences	C
General Biology (Lab Guide—1960, 1961)	Biological Sciences	C
Botany (1957)	Biological Sciences	C
Plant Kingdom (1962—Botany)	Biological Sciences	C
Lab Guide for Zoology (3rd Ed., 1957)	Biological Sciences	C
Introductory Mycology (1952, 1962)	Biological Sciences	C
Beginning Synchronized Swimming (2nd Ed., 1958)	Physical Education	S, C

APPLETON-CENTURY CROFTS
34 West 33 Street
New York 1, New York

Book	*Subject Area*	*Grade Level*
Programmed Vocabulary	English & Speech	S, C

McGRAW-HILL BOOK CO., INC.
GREGG DIVISION
330 West 42 Street
New York 36, New York

College Accounting *Theory and Practice*	Business	C

McGRAW-HILL BOOK CO., INC.
WEBSTER DIVISION
1154 Reco Avenue
St. Louis 26, Missouri

J'Etudie Le Francais *A La Maison et A L'Ecole*	Modern Foreign Language	E

Index

Index

A

Abstract symbolism, 75
Adhesive-backed coloring film, 25
Algebra, 65
Alyea T.O.P.S. experiment, 33
Ancient history, 116, 119
Art, use of overhead projection in, 189-214

B

Basal reader, 80
Beginning sounds, 77
Biology, 33, 34
Bookkeeping, 184, 187
Business education, use of overhead projection in, 175-188
Business law, 179
Business letters, 110, 183

C

Carpentry, 168
Cartooning, 97, 164, 179
Chemistry, 37
Color-lift process, 8, 25, 84, 129, 194, 200
Consonants, 88
Copying machines (see infrared copying machine and white-light copying machine)
Crafts, 198

D

Diagramming, 103
Dictionary skills, 105
Direct reading image negative film, 24
Direct reading image positive film, 22
Drafting, 157, 164
Drama, 103
Drawing, portrait and figure, 199

E

Earth science, 37
Ebacher method, 146
Economics, 179
Electronics, 166
Engine mechanics, 161
Entomology, 51
European history, 121
Eye movement, in reading, 84

F

Football, 216, 219
Foreign languages, use of overhead projection in, 134-152